Secrets of Creating a Green Business

Retail, Wholesale, Internet

Secrets
of Creating
a Green Business

Retail, Wholesale, Internet

DOROTHY FINELL

CONTENTS

ACKNOWLEDGEMENTS

Many thanks go to editor Hollie Davies for her tireless efforts to keep things on track. Her guidance was valuable beyond belief. Also, my most heartfelt, grateful thanks and appreciation go to Lori Oliver and Nancy Fasulo who were there for me when I really needed their help. Warm thanks go to Pat Mueller-Vollmer for her invaluable contribution.

Finally, I extend my greatest appreciation to all the company and store owners or managers who gave so graciously of their valuable time to share their success stories and impart their knowledge, often in great depth, during the interviews.

Thank you, all of you.

ABOUT THE AUTHOR

Dorothy Finell is the author of The Specialty Shop: How To Create Your Own Unique and Profitable Retail Business (Amacom 2007). To complete Secrets of Creating a Green Business: Retail, Wholesale and Internet she traveled parts of the world conducting interviews with successful green business owners.

Dorothy has twenty years of retail experience as the owner of specialty shops, and co-owner of the oldest department store in the United States where she was a buyer, merchandise manager, window designer, and personnel director. She served on the Board of Directors of the Connecticut Retail Merchants Association, in addition to having her own radio show.

Dorothy, who resides in Carmel, California, is also the author of the award-winning book, *Finally Home: Five Lives in One*, a collection of personal memoirs which she wrote solely for charitable purposes and all proceeds go to the Marvin Finell Fund at the Connecticut Children's Medical Center School (for brain-damaged children). She is the mother of seven children.

Prior to her retail career, she taught writing at Hanover High School and Dartmouth College.

STATISTICS

230 million

Tons of refuse each American produces a year—or 5.1 pounds per person every day. (www.enotes.com)

3.6 billion

Gallons of crude oil needed to produce tires for all passenger cars in the United States—or 7 gallons of crude oil per tire. (www.encyclopedia.com)

30

Days (average) before recycled glass bottles reappear on the store shelf. (www.gpi.org)

60

Pounds of air pollutants a single tree filters in a year. (www.recyclextreme.com)

1,590

Pounds of carbon dioxide reduction a year you could achieve by leaving your car at home two days a week (walking, biking or taking the bus instead) (www.thedailygreen.com)

1 trillion

The higher of estimates for the number of plastic bags consumed worldwide in a year. That's more than 1 million per minute. Billions become litter each year. The United States consumes more than 380 billion plastic bags, sacks and wraps every year. Shopping bags represent 100 billion of those. The estimated cost to retailers: $4 billion. (www.reusablebags.com

GLOSSARY

- *Green:* the all-encompassing term often used to suggest the environmentally sensitive way of living, and in this book, of doing business.

- *To Go Green:* to make a conscious effort to conserve resources and protect the environment.

- *Biodegradable:* waste materials able to be broken down with the help of microorganisms into inert waste.

- *Carbon footprint:* the impact of a person or industry on the world environment calculated by measuring carbon dioxide emission equivalents.

- *Carbon neutrality:* a net zero balance of greenhouse gas emissions and offsets.

- *Compostable:* waste materials able to be broken down into a nutritive material capable of supporting plant life.

- *Eco-friendly:* products made with a healthy environment in mind whether during manufacture, distribution, use or disposal.

- *Organic:* produced without genetic modification, irradiation or synthetic additives including preservatives, chemicals, solvents, or fertilizers, unless from animal and/or vegetable sources (including insects and microorganisms).

- *Recycle:* to convert waste material from its original state into a state that can be remanufactured into another product whether like-kind or entirely dissimilar; for example, glass jars crushed and made into wall tiles.

- *Reduce:* to lessen, limit, or entirely eliminate disposable products and packaging resulting in an overall reduction in the need for waste transport and disposal.

- *Repurpose:* to use a product for something other than its originally intended purpose; for example, using a glass jar as a drinking glass, vase, or storage container.

- *Reuse:* to use a single product for successive uses; for example, an empty pickle jar used to make or store pickles. Note: Reusing and repurposing contribute greatly towards the reduction of waste.

- *Sustainable:* products or actions that meet current needs without sacrificing the ability of a future generation to meet its needs.

- *Upcycle:* to convert waste materials or useless products into useful products or new materials of better quality or of a higher environmental value.

PRIMARY PRINCIPLES OF RETAILING

1. The Right Item, at the Right Price, in the Right Place at the Right Time

2. An abundance and variety of stock

3. Listen, listen, listen to your customers

4. The customer is always right

5. You cannot be everything to everybody

6. Not every item will be a winner

7. Respect your customers

8. Be honest with your customers—do not tell them you can do something you cannot

9. Do not make excuses to your customers

10. Do not take for granted that your salespeople should know something

11. There is only one chance to build an excellent reputation

12. Your salespeople represent you and your reputation

13. Your marketing budget should be largest in tough economic times

14. Attend as many trade shows, expos and fairs as possible

15. Do not be greedy in pricing

Use your imagination!

Adapted from: The Specialty Shop: How to Create Your Own Unique and Profitable Retail Business, AMACOM Books ©2007 Dorothy Finell, edited by Hollie Davies.

INTRODUCTION

This book is about business—green business.

As more people change their lifestyle to a natural, sustainable way of life, a "green" way has emerged and become mainstream in the last few years. The basics of life for everyone are never changing: a roof over their heads, food in their stomachs, and clothes on their backs

Likewise, corporations, and large and small companies have adapted to a green way of business instituting policies that affect everything from lighting to trash. From grocery chains to drug corporations, furniture stores to clothing shops, the mainstream business world has become largely green.

☞

The major areas for starting up a green business or converting an existing one to green included in this book:

- ✒ Start Ups cover online and on-site business models

- ✒ Business Administration includes various methods of financing

- ✒ Marketing covers public relations, advertising, trade shows and internet marketing.

Also included are twenty-one face-to-face interviews with owners of successful businesses; a brief history of raw materials; and the evolution of green business.

Hemp and bamboo are perhaps the two oldest natural living materials in the world. Over a thousand years ago, countless items were made from them. The evolution of these materials' use in the production of consumer goods today is astonishing; in fact, the number exceeds a thousand with more in experimental stages.

CHAPTER I

HEMP

The history of hemp in the United States is astounding—as are the products, byproducts and applications for new products. Hemp has more than 25,000 known uses today in categories that include food, fuel, clothing, oil, housing, paper and textiles. It is the oldest cultivated fiber plant in the world.

One acre of hemp is equal to the usable fibers of four acres of trees or two acres of cotton, and hemp takes four months or less to grow on most farmland. From a production standpoint, hemp is a dream compared to most other crops. The fiber, stronger than steel but softer than cotton, withstands frost, heat, mildew and insects, and therefore requires little or no herbicides, pesticides or fungicides. It requires only moderate amounts of fertilizer and water, yet is unaffected by too much or too little water, and goes undamaged by light. Due to this durability, paper products made from hemp have incredible longevity, yet are biodegradable.

Paper made from rags containing hemp fiber does not yellow and can last for centuries. Examples—in the United States alone—bibles, maps, charts, stocks, bonds, newspapers, paper money, and the first drafts of the Declaration of Independence and United States Constitution. Many of the world's greatest artists, including Rembrandt and Van Gogh, painted on hemp linen canvases that have lasted hundreds of years.

There are three categories of hemp:

- varieties cultivated for fiber, known as industrial hemp

1

ع varieties grown for seeds and oil

ع varieties grown for medicinal or drug use

The last category is comprised of three groups of cannabis; only one is illegal—the variety that produces marijuana or hashish, which contains THC (delta-9-tetrahydrocannabinol), the active ingredient in marijuana, the psychoactive ingredient, with levels as high as 30 percent.

But the varieties grown for industrial fiber, seeds and oil contain THC limits of only 0.3 percent in the European Union, 1 percent for Canada, and somewhere in between in the United States.

The industrial variety of cannabis can produce large quantities of paper, textiles, building materials, food, paint, varnish, oil, ink and fuel.

Native Americans grew hemp and, until 1937, the resource continued to be a major U.S. crop utilized for textiles, fabrics, linens, drapes, clothing, and export to other countries. The War of 1812, between England and America, had several complex causes, but one aspect of the war was due to U.S. exports of hemp to France, which was warring with England.

Hemp was grown by poor and rich alike: President George Washington grew hemp. Thomas Jefferson smuggled hemp seeds from China to America, and he too grew hemp. Benjamin Franklin owned one of the first paper mills to process hemp. Henry Ford's first Model-T was constructed from hemp and built to run on hemp gasoline. Ford also built a "plastic" car made of hemp and wheat straw, which would have been biodegradable.

In the 1820s, the cotton gin was introduced and hemp sales dropped sharply as the same items made from hemp became all the rage in cotton, which cost less. Despite the popularity of cotton, hemp was still considered so versatile that in 1916 the U.S. government predicted that by the 1940s all paper would be made from hemp. Plans were made to stop trees from being felled.

Mechanical Engineering Magazine (February 1938) published "The Most Popular and Desirable Crop That Can Be Grown," an article stating that if hemp were cultivated using 20th century technology, it would be the single largest agricultural crop in the United States and the rest of the world. Others predicted it could be the first cash crop that could exceed a billion dollars. In the 1930s, hemp could have generated thousands of new products. These innovations, the single resource that could have created millions of new jobs, would have lifted the country from the Depression. Yet by 1937 hemp was all but illegal in the United States, and today it is illegal for U.S. farmers to grow hemp.

What happened?

In hindsight, the history of U.S. hemp production seems shockingly shortsighted; a victim of politics and possible collusion—as many historians have suggested—by a group of influential men who had a vested interest in ending hemp production. Several factors came together at the same time to decide hemp's fate. William Randolph Hearst and the Hearst Paper Manufacturing Division of Kimberly Clark owned many thousands of timberland acres for paper production. Hemp paper products competed with Hearst's tree-based paper products. If the paper made from trees had been replaced by paper made from hemp, Hearst would have been ruined.

Another powerful man, DuPont of E.I. DuPont, had patented a variety of synthetic materials from oil and coal, producing many products that competed with those made of hemp.

According to various historical sources, E.I. DuPont urged its stockholders and business associates to invest in its new petrochemical industry of plastics, cellophane, celluloid, nylon, rayon, Dacron, methanol and other synthetics, resulting in many hemp-based products being replaced by synthetic-based products.

Meanwhile, Andrew Mellon, often referred to as a "robber baron" and DuPont's number one investor, became President Hoover's Secretary of the Treasury and appointed a close relative to head the Federal Bureau of Narcotics and Dangerous Drugs.

The group of tycoons held secret meetings where they decided that from then on hemp would be considered a dangerous drug. They renamed it "marihuana" (as it was spelled then), a Mexican slang word. Hearst's various newspapers began publishing racist headlines to a frightened public about Mexican, Negro, and Caucasian criminals committing "vile and disgusting acts" while under the influence of marihuana.

By 1937, the onslaught of attacks against hemp from so many influential sources resulted in Congress passing The Marihuana Act, declaring cannabis and marihuana illegal. Even though industrial hemp was completely different from the cannabis used as a drug, it too was part of the sweeping ban. Anyone producing hemp products eventually had to import hemp from the Philippines and other countries.

However, the government had to backtrack during WWII. It needed vast amounts of hemp products for the war, but after Japan invaded the Philippines, U.S. hemp imports dried up. The government began vigorously encouraging hemp farming, even producing a film called Hemp for Victory. But the movement was short-lived, and after the war, as plastics and synthetics gained huge popularity, U.S. hemp farming virtually disappeared.

The final act against hemp production came in 1970, when the Controlled Substances Act made it illegal to grow hemp without a Drug Enforcement Agency permit. The move— made during the Nixon administration's war on drugs— outraged opponents of the CSA, because the law made no distinction between cannabis plants that produce industrial hemp and cannabis that produces the marijuana variety. All hemp production technically became illegal.

Literally millions of wild hemp plants grow throughout the country, and these have low THC content, no drug potential, but cannot be harvested for industrial purposes.

Since that time, U.S. manufacturers of hemp products have been buying from countries where hemp crops represent multimillion-dollar industries. Canada, Australia, Great Britain, Russia, China, and much of Europe have thriving hemp industries.

Today, Hemp Industries Association, which represents more than 200 North American hemp companies, won a protracted lawsuit against the DEA in a decision that blocked regulations banning hemp foods. The case established that hemp foods would be exempt from the Controlled Substances Act. The ruling excludes hemp seed and oil from the same controls as hemp fiber, clearing the way to sell hemp seed and hemp oil food products.

Due to its highly nutritious components, hemp products and byproducts will become increasingly important in United States food and beauty care markets, resulting in an increase of these products in vitamin shops, organic food stores, bakeries and restaurants and the cosmetics industry.

Hemp seeds are more nutritious and economical to produce than soybeans. Both contain protein. Hemp seed protein can be used to produce any product made from soybeans (tofu, butter, cheese, salad oils, ice cream, milk and more). Hemp seed can also be ground into a flour to produce pasta, cookies and breads. Hemp oil contains the highest amount of fatty acids from any plant. The byproduct of pressed hemp seed oil is protein seed 'cake'; when ground, this can also be used to bake cakes and breads. Because hemp seed protein—the most complete vegetable protein in the plant kingdom—and the oils contained therein, are rich in lanolin, the latter is increasingly used in body care products.

The Hemp Industries Association estimates North American sales of industrial hemp products in 2008 to have been $360 million.

As of 2009, 16 states have passed pro-hemp legislation and/or are taking legal steps toward production, using the same strict restrictions 'in place' in Canada. These states include Colorado, North Dakota, Hawaii, Kentucky, Maine,

New Mexico, Maryland, Montana, Oregon, Vermont and West Virginia. Even though these states have passed legislation allowing hemp production, they still cannot go into effect until the DEA lifts its ban.

As of this writing, 28 states have introduced hemp legislation; 16 bills became law, but eight more—Hawaii, Kentucky, Maine, Maryland, Montana, New Mexico, North Dakota, Vermont and West Virginia—have removed barriers to its production or research and have also enacted laws. (www.votehemp.com)

Hemp is and will be used to manufacture biofuels in addition to biodegradable plastic substitutes called bioplastics. It is already being used in the manufacturing of paper—tissue paper, cardboard, stationery and wrapping. The hemp clothing industry—together with the re-emergence of the bed and bath linens industry—was reborn in 1988 with the rediscovery of hemp fiber production. Thousands of products can and will be produced from hemp in the years to come: from tools to musical instruments, from scales to CDs. With 21st century green technology, the potential could be limitless for durable yet biodegradable hemp products.

If and when industrial hemp production is again legalized in the United States, entrepreneurs interested in producing hemp-based products can look forward to a tremendous market potential.

∽

While the two most important green materials—hemp and bamboo—are emphasized here, others, like organic cotton and cork, are mentioned in lesser detail. Nonetheless, it is important for you, the prospective entrepreneur, to know about the various materials involved in the manufacture of green products because how is one able to create green products without an intimate knowledge of those materials? Retailers, as well, need to know and understand materials and manufacturing techniques because if, for example, a customer can only wear organic cotton, which is manufactured differently from regular cotton, that customer is relying on the owner/retailer/salesperson to know that information.

It is likewise important to consider the countries from which the products and materials are shipped. What is the carbon footprint associated with the product or raw material? Generally speaking, the greater the distance, the greater the carbon footprint. Also, shipping costs will be higher, possibly making your green product, while superior in certain ways, non-competitive with a similar non-green product.

In the ideal scenario, products manufactured from local, sustainable raw materials will satisfy your green goals, keep costs down, and allow for competitive pricing.

THE HEMP GALLERY

Hemp goes far deeper than "hippie" culture. In fact, says Ray Rankin of Hemp Gallery in Sydney, Australia, "Levi's jeans were originally made from recycled hemp canvas because it was so strong. Sailing ships brought immigrants to the United States, and while in the States, the ships were refitted with hemp-made sails for their return trip."

The Rankins, Ray and Beatrice, are caring people. Until a few years ago, Ray was a builder and Beatrice a concert pianist. Now they are the owners of Hemp Gallery in Sydney, where they manufacture, distribute, wholesale and retail hemp products. They feel passionately about the material and its by-products, and even more about their role in the greening of the environment.

"For both Ray and me," Beatrice remarks, "Australia is our adopted home and we love it. I grew up in the Middle East, and I love the freedom and purity of Australia as a whole, whereas Ray, as a New Zealander, loves the warm climate, so protecting our environment was the main reason for our business." The Rankins chose hemp because they appreciate the fact that one plant can provide all the basics for human survival: food, clothing, shelter and energy (hemp fuel, biomass) "without harming our beautiful Earth."

Hemp is one of the most generous plant fibers on the planet, because almost every aspect of it can be utilized for widely differing end products. The Rankins allow none of hemp's amazing qualities to go to waste, creating fabrics, linens, hemp seed oil, hemp-seed meal, rope and twine, cosmetics and baby products.

Hemp Gallery stocks a variety of hemp fabrics:

- Hemp rolls, made in Laos

- Hemp-blend fabrics, such as hemp combined with yak hair, resulting in a soft, yet strong, silk-like fabric

- Hemp and silk blend

- Hemp and organic cotton blend

- Hemp and PET blend (polyethylene terephthalate from recycled plastic bottles)

Hemp/PET blend fabric consists of 55 percent hemp fiber and 45 percent PET fiber and respun with hemp to create a new environmental version of poly/cotton fabric. The blends are manufactured in China (although Ray is finding an Australian source) and suitable for blinds, curtains and upholstery, as well as certain types of clothing.

Soft, luxurious bedding is one of many end products derived from hemp, possibly the most generous plant fiber on Earth.

One of the Rankins' specialties is their bedding fabric, a linen comprised of 55 percent hemp and 45 percent certified raw cotton fiber that softens with each wash. Manufactured in China and distributed by The Hemp Gallery, the bed linens are one color only, a light tan. They initially offered many colors, but Beatrice observes, "Everyone seemed to want slightly different shades of the colors," so they stopped offering a variety, even though hemp takes dyes well. "The "natural color" of the blended fabric looks elegant and feels beautifully soft and smooth," Beatrice adds.

Another end product of hemp is hemp-seed oil, widely used in green beauty products. The Rankins' Australian-grown, premium food-grade quality hemp seed oil is cold pressed below 40 degrees, nitrogen flushed, and sealed in drums at a certified organic facility. The "handcrafted" hemp seed oil is the natural ingredient in their soaps, hair care and body products. All products, excluding the unscented soap, are scented with 100 percent natural essential oils that contain a high content of Omega 3, Omega 6 and Omega 9, along with vitamins B1, B2, B3, B6, C, D and E, calcium, chlorophyll, iron, magnesium, phosphorus, potassium and zinc.

Yet another by-product of hemp is hemp-seed meal, the material that remains after the oil is extracted from the seeds. The hemp-seed meal is marketed either as is (a coarse meal used for baking and as pet food supplement) or ground and milled to produce a fine flour, usually packaged and sold as a protein powder/nutritional supplement. The Rankins shared a couple of their popular and delicious hemp-seed meal recipes:

HEMP FRIDGE FUDGE

    1 cup almond meal
    1/2 cup desiccated coconut
    2 tbsp. hemp protein powder
    1/2 cup tahini, unhulled
    1/2 cup cocoa or light carob powder
    1 tbsp. dark agave syrup (to sweeten)
    1/3 cup melted coconut oil
    1/2 cup roasted blanched almonds or rice puffs (optional)

Melt coconut oil in a saucepan, if necessary. Combine all ingredients in a bowl. The mix should be the consistency of peanut paste. If it's too dry, add a little more coconut oil. Press mixture into square shallow dish (Beatrice uses a glass Pyrex dish). Sprinkle with desiccated coconut and refrigerate until it sets (a couple of hours). This mix can be put into waxed mini cup cake containers for a single serve.

BANANA BREAD WITH HEMP FLOUR AND HAZELNUT AGAVE SYRUP

1/2 cup hemp flour
1/3 cup sunflower oil
2 cups plain flour
1/2 cup hazelnut agave syrup
1 tsp. baking soda
2-3 mashed bananas
1/4 tsp. salt
2 eggs

Mix dry ingredients in a bowl. Mix wet ingredients in another bowl. Combine wet and dry ingredients, add chopped nuts (optional). Hazelnut agave syrup can be replaced with 1/3 cup milk and hazelnut essence or 1/3 cup molasses. Pour into loaf pan. Bake for one hour at 350 °F or until fork comes out clean.

∽

Perhaps the best-known use for hemp is for ropes and twines. It is the only fiber that strengthens when wet. Polished twine is used to string necklaces and bracelets, as twine knots easily and holds securely without requiring glue. The Rankins sell to a variety of manufacturers.

Hemp is fast becoming a major ingredient in a variety of "green" baby products: Australian-designed hemp diapers and Australian-made diaper liners, baby wraps and soap are a few of the baby products that Hemp Gallery distributes.

Most people are aware that hashish and hash oil—illegal substances—can also be derived from hemp, although it's not a product at Hemp Gallery.

Beatrice relates a story of a long-time client—a happy, cheerful person who had heard about the benefits of organic hemp seed oil and wanted to try it out.

"After a few weeks, she came back to the stand where we sold organic products on weekends and announced in a loud voice, in front of a large crowd of customers, that every day for the prior three weeks, she had absolutely loved eating, drinking, and rubbing this wonderful hash oil all over her body. You can imagine our embarrassment!"

For new ideas and marketing exposure, the Rankins attend designEX, decoration and design trade shows—basically for architects and interior and exterior designers—in addition to the Reed Gift Fair. The Rankins find trade shows productive for meeting new buyers and manufacturers in the green world, and also for networking with new clients and taking orders for products. They also sell certain products at weekend markets, which they attend regularly. "Because hemp is so misunderstood among the general public," Ray says, "it's good to get out and meet the people one-on-one to inform them in the relaxed market environment."

Approximately 50 percent of their sales are wholesale and 50 percent retail (through the markets, Internet, and direct sales from their showroom). Despite recessionary conditions, the Rankins report increased sales. Since doing Trade Fairs aimed at designers and architects, they have focused mainly on wholesaling hemp fabric, hemp bed linen, and hemp conference bags.

The company currently manufactures bed linen, print designs on fabric, soft furnishings such as cushion covers, curtains, baby wraps, and teething dolls, using imported fabrics. Customized designs and a custom-made drapery service—including free measurements—are part of the company's personalized service, which also includes decorator consultations.

The Rankins financed the business start-up using only their savings, but their advice for new retailers is to secure enough financial backing, through bank loans or other sources, for two years.

They run their business with the help of two office staff and a graphic artist/web designer. They also employ an on-call business consultant.

Beatrice is so intent on spreading the word about sustainability and promoting a completely green environment that she accepts all speaking engagements that come her way, which has become part of marketing and public relations. She envisions a larger goal than their business' success: to know that she is, in her own small way, "making a difference."

The Rankins' long-term goal is to grow and process hemp on their own land and distribute and export it "from seed to store." But in the nearer term, in a few years, they hope to develop a range of green textiles and fabrics for bed linens, soft furnishings—all kinds of pillows and accessories—carpets and rugs. Or, as they say, "Create one-stop shopping of hemp-based products for interior designers as well as for retail."

And some time in between, they have an idea they hope will come to fruition: Any product made of wood today will be replaced tomorrow by hemp, including their much-loved musical instruments.

Hemp Gallery
PO Box 84
Belrose, NSW 2085
Australia
Phone: +61.2 8901 0375
Fax: +61.2 9975 6762
info@hempgallery.com.au
www.hempgallery.com.au

THE NATURAL BEDDING COMPANY

"Natural bedding is so-called because mattresses and bed frames are made from natural materials: wood, bamboo, hemp, cotton, wool, latex and coconut coir that have neutral electric properties and are therefore recommended by Building Biologists all over the world."

Paul Hermann, B.Sc., Dip. Ed.
Certified Building Biologist
Leura, New South Wales, Australia

The Natural Bedding Company, owned by Andrew McCaig, is a manufacturer, wholesaler and retailer of natural mattresses, bed frames, pillows, and accessories. At his shop/factory in Sydney, Australia, Andrew manufactures approximately 125 items, including adult mattresses, children's cots and bassinets, futons, sofa beds and frames, woolen doonas (duvets), and natural latex and wool overlays (bed coverings).

Andrew is committed to doing his part in saving the environment and states his philosophy unequivocally: "We are not a mainstream business and have created a stress-free environment where a person can lie down, for hours if necessary, to determine which is the right mattress for him or her." A dedicated environmentalist, he added: "We encourage customers to think critically and ethically about their individual needs in relation to bedding products before they consider purchasing from anyone, including us."

Andrew's products are designed for maximum customer health, while causing minimum environmental impact. They are particularly in demand by customers with chemical sensitivities and allergies, and Natural Bedding was a finalist in the Marrickville Council Sustainability & Eco Awards.

Natural Bedding manufactures a range of natural latex mattresses: those made with hemp or wool, among others, and their Cloud mattresses are becoming extremely popular. They are constructed of cotton, wool, naturally rubberized coconut fiber (coir) and natural latex; the latter—which is anti-bacterial, antifungal, and dust mite-resistant—is pure latex foam produced from plantation rubber trees grown in Malaysia, and composed of 98 percent unadulterated natural rubber sap with the remaining 2 percent comprised of tree minerals and salts— organic components—all of which turn the sap into foam. Untreated downs wool from Australia is sustainable, biodegradable, non-allergenic and is a natural flame retardant.

Finally, a layer of ripple latex allows another supportive layer to be adapted for further comfort. Because bedsprings are not eco-friendly, NBC eliminates those altogether. The natural coverings of the mattresses are made from their own organic cotton/hemp combination. Andrew emphasizes that all of their natural materials are tested and analyzed.

Sustainable woods, such as Australian ash and pine, are used for bed frames and other furniture items. The wood is purchased from Good Wood, a private company that adheres to the (Australian) Eco Select program of stringent regulations regarding regeneration processes for felling and replanting trees. Frame bases require a minimal amount of water-based glue, and customers are encouraged to oil the frames rather than applying synthetic stains. Oils used are Ardvos, a nontoxic green oil from the tung tree. "We refuse to use the topic chemicals and synthetics (nonessential polypropylenes, Dacron, nylons and synthetic foams) that mainstream manufacturers use."

Andrew's design research has been guided in part by his customer's questions and needs. Chiropractors and physiotherapists who bought beds for themselves were so impressed that they now sell NBC beds to their patients.

Wood chips from the majority of hardwood trees are the end product and sell for a low price per ton. According to Andrew, wood chips are exported to other countries for manufacturing paper. It takes two tons of chips to make one ton of paper.

Andrew estimates his sales at 50 percent retail and 30 percent wholesale. Twenty percent are donations to charities, such as Make a Wish Foundation, Diabetes Australia, and other civic projects.

Bed frames are made of sustainable woods, such as Australian Ash, and customers are encouraged to oil the frame rather than apply synthetic stains.

When he started his business 24 years ago with only his savings, he worked alone in the front room of his house, with two bales of cotton to make his mattresses. He now employs five people who manufacture the items in the back room of his shop and at another location, where the mattresses are packed in biodegradable plastic. The retail shop is 250 square meters (2,690.9 square feet) and the mattress manufacturing area, 150 square meters (1614.6 square feet). The woodwork factory is 300 square meters (3228.1 square feet), and the storage facility is 200 square meters (2152.8 square feet). The locations total 900 square meters (9,687.5 square feet).

Despite his company's growth, he would not dream of borrowing money.

Most of his employees have been members of the student body at Sydney University. "This allows young people with a need for income to gain experience in the operations of a small business while contributing their own individual skills," Andrew explains.

Andrew offers sales twice a year for existing and new customers, who receive notices of sales, special offers, and a newsletter through his website. The website, he notes, has paid the best dividends through the years and is the only marketing tool he uses.

Bamboo, like hemp, is a very strong, dust mite-resistant, long-lasting fiber that requires little water and no pesticides, and grows wild in many places. "We are looking into the costs of building bed frames with bamboo," says Andrew, who's researching Australian sources for bamboo and for a processor using a guaranteed environmentally sound process.

When the author, intrigued with Andrew's statement about "customers trying out beds for hours," asked for more information, Andrew replied:

"One afternoon, a handsome young man came in looking for a mattress. He lay down on several for about three hours while flirting with the female staff, and stayed until 5:00 p.m., so the shop had technically closed. A woman passing by the shop window stopped and looked in, and the man, still lying on a bed, waved to her. At 5:05 p.m., the shop telephone rang and a woman's voice said, 'I don't want to appear forward, but can I speak to the man lying on the bed in your window?' Being a helpful salesman, I handed the phone to my potential customer and they proceeded to chat for 10 minutes. He finally left, giving us all kisses and saying he'd be back. About two weeks later he returned and bought a queen-size bed and mattress. We inquired about the woman on the phone; had they spoken again? 'Yes,' he said, and sheepishly, revealing that he was now dating her."

The Natural Bedding Company

122 Percival Road
Stanmore, Sydney, 2048
Phone: (02) 9569-4834
Fax: (02) 9564-6242
natbed@iprimus.com.au
www.naturalbedding.com.au

CHAPTER 2

BAMBOO

A ncient. Versatile. Life-sustaining and sustainable. Bamboo has a history dating back several thousand years to ancient China, but never has it been more at the forefront of the world's economy, now that going green has gained global importance. Bamboo has more than 1,000 applications. You could subsist a lifetime on only the products of bamboo, which never stops growing.

Harvesting, processing and manufacture of bamboo products create jobs, income, food, fuel, clothing, and housing for more than 2.5 billion people worldwide. So vast are the byproducts and end uses that the planet could subsist on bamboo alone for essential needs. Fortunately for future supplies, there are more than 1,200 species of bamboo, which is native to every inhabited continent except Europe. Like hemp, almost every part of bamboo can be sourced for a growing number of applications—as fast as designers and entrepreneurs imagine them.

This evergreen material belongs to the grass family and has long played an important role in history: In China, the earliest writing paper, food, medicine and eating utensils were made from bamboo. Bamboo provided the first re-greening after the 1945 atomic blast in Hiroshima. And Thomas Edison used carbonized bamboo for the first light-bulb filament.

Strong and durable, bamboo has been used for centuries as building material in many Asian countries; its toughness makes bamboo ideal to help earthquake-proof buildings. Belying its strength, however, bamboo is also remarkably flexible. Many qualities unique to bamboo make it ideal for a greening society:

- Bamboo is the fastest-growing plant on the planet— some species at the rate of 47 inches a day. Many bamboo "forests" tower higher than 100 feet.

- Bamboo is a sustainable replacement for wood.

- Bamboo tolerates extreme temperature conditions.

- A grove of bamboo releases 35 percent more oxygen than an equivalent grove of trees.

- Bamboo is one of the top soil-conservation elements that greatly reduces rain runoff and prevents widespread soil erosion.

- New shoots of bamboo provide a variety of food and medicinal products.

- Bamboo provides heating fuel.

- Bamboo fibers are used to create fabric for clothing.

In the United States, bamboo grows best in soil along the banks of rivers or creeks. The Southeast produces the only native species, commonly called River Cane. It also grows from Maryland as far west as Missouri and as far south as Texas, including Florida. It is native, however, to China. Japanese Timber bamboo is China derivative. Black bamboo is a related species of Hennon bamboo and actually black in color.

Fishing poles are made from Fishpole bamboo, along with Golden bamboo, which is also used for walking sticks and poles. Yellow Groove bamboo, as its name implies, sports a bright yellow groove and grows as far north as Massachusetts. All of these varieties have two common qualities: they are hardy to 15 degrees below zero (Fahrenheit) and their native habitat is the Yangtze River Valley in China. One variety, Fountain bamboo, grows in the mountains of China where the temperature is so cold it can still thrive at 10 degrees below zero. But in the U.S. Southeast, the temperature is unlikely to reach such lows.

Two Chinese varieties have been cultivated in Japan for centuries, and each country calls them by different names. Madake in Japan is called Moso in China. Experts consider Moso one of the world's most beautiful bamboos, and it is one of the most widely grown in China. Because of the height of its leaves, pandas do not favor this variety; therefore, it remains untouched and intact.

We cannot list the thousands of bamboo products here, but the material is being widely used in many industries for myriad products, including:

- housewares and tableware
- automotive
- cosmetics
- food and beverage
- men's, women's and children's clothing
- jewelry
- clothing accessories
- packaging/books/paper products
- construction/fencing/flooring/carpeting
- kitchen utensils
- bathroom accessories
- carpeting
- musical instruments
- gardening and horticultural
- pharmaceuticals
- sporting goods

Chinese medicine uses bamboo products extensively to treat a variety of maladies, including kidney disease, venereal disease, and prickly heat. Chinese herbs, many derived from different parts of bamboo, also treat numerous ailments in the United States, Europe, and other countries. Some are prescribed by holistic doctors, others are recommended and dispensed by chiropractors, osteopaths and even massage therapists. Vitamin and herb shops carry the products.

One of the most interesting uses for bamboo is in eco-friendly clothing. Bamboo is the magic ingredient in textile fibers from which viscose fiber is derived. The fiber itself is 100 percent biodegradable. New processing equipment enables bamboo pulp—once considered a waste product—to be turned into yarn. Bamboo fabric feels like silk or cashmere; it's softer than any cotton and absorbs water about four times better than cotton. Many manufacturers state that bamboo clothing is naturally temperature regulated, anti-static and anti-fungal due to an agent that prevents bacteria cultivation, and offers UV protection.

Some parts of bamboo have been used in cooking for centuries. Certain types of bamboo shoots are protein rich and contain vitamins, sugar and fat. Antioxidant properties of pulverized bamboo bark prevent bacterial growth and are used as a natural food preservative. Wherever they are found fresh, shoots are used in cooking—from fine restaurants to neighborhood cafes, and particularly in Chinatowns in cities such as San Francisco, Los Angeles and New York, as well as farmers markets in the Southeast.

Food is one of the three basic needs of life, and bamboo—in the form of shoots and rice—offers every course, from breakfast to dinner, to sustain a person throughout the day.

Some of my favorites include bamboo rice mixed with fruit and honey for breakfast. A stir-fry of pork, bamboo shoots and vegetables; baked bamboo shoots and cheese; chicken soup with bamboo shoots and bamboo rice; or a salad of bamboo rice with apples, ginger and cheese make a fine lunch. And dinners include pork braised with bamboo shoots in soy sauce; coconut shrimp with ginger bamboo rice; spinach with bamboo shoots and rice; and corned beef and bamboo rice stuffed cabbage or ginger pork, vegetables and bamboo rice cakes. For dessert: cinnamon currant bamboo rice with honey, bamboo rice cakes with ginger sauce and kumquats, or coconut bamboo rice pudding. With only two bamboo foods, a host of recipes emerges.

Bamboo certainly factors into the planet's future and, therefore, entrepreneurs should consider its applications when starting an eco-business. Scores of countries around the world have bamboo industries and thousands of websites related to bamboo offer a wealth of information about its history, properties and, most importantly, its potential.

BAMBU

Jeff Delkin and Rachael Speth are in the right business, in the right place, at the right time, with the right material: bamboo. They are manufacturers, retailers, wholesalers, designers, and creators of products—and wear a host of other hats as well. Their business name? bambu.

The unusual aspect of their partnership is that Rachael and Jeff are Americans living and working in Shanghai, China. Prior to that, they traveled for 2½ years to Japan, Nepal, Australia and China to learn everything they could about bamboo. They met with craftspeople, academics, growers and government people, and attended the workshops of International Network of Bamboo and Rattan. Previously, they lived and worked in New York City, where each climbed the ladder of success: Rachael in product development at Nike; Jeff in marketing and advertising at Ogilvy & Mather.

They left their large companies with a great deal of experience because they wanted their own business. They found, in Asia, that bamboo is as "green" a raw material—along with hemp—as exists, and that they were practically sitting on top of it in China, the world's largest supplier. They knew they had found their niche and could apply their combined experience into a company. In 2003, they started bambu.

They found an office near their home where they could walk to work, thereby reducing their carbon footprint. Having researched bamboo for 2½ years, they chose moso bamboo to create their products. Moso, native to China, is plentiful, hardy and considered one of the world's most beautiful (culms, or stalks, are a bluish-green color) and is the most abundant of

27

bamboos. As with all bamboo, it does not require replanting when cut; it renews itself. It grows as a "wild" crop from an elaborate root system. The moso bamboo used by bambu is sustainably grown, harvested and managed by local farmers.

Bambu then either purchases directly from the farmers or from a factory that produces bamboo laminates (strips cut into equal shapes and lengths and adhered together to create a uniform surface). It is beautiful and, equally important, pandas seldom eat it, so it is also plentiful and in pristine condition.

Every aspect of an eco-green existence is important to Jeff and Rachael, so first and foremost they developed the principals to which they would adhere—they would be responsible manufacturers with a focus on:

- Workers—their health and safety

- Fair wages—for all their teams

- Environment—protection of land

They demand, in turn, that their manufacturing partners meet their standards of quality craftsmanship. Jeff points out that as a result of their Fair Trade practices they were granted the Co-op America Seal of Approval.

Rachael and Jeff, as owners of bambu, intentionally located themselves at the center of production; they live and work among their producer groups. Their team is composed of Quality Control Managers who work with each of six production centers; four in China and two in Vietnam. The managers are trained to oversee production from beginning to the final output. Every order is supervised and approved by people bambu employs. Another team works on product development and production at their office in Shanghai.

The production centers, each of which makes a different product, are comprised of the various producer groups with whom Rachael works; starting with the wood cutters who cut the bamboo culm (the technical term for a bamboo tree or stalk) into consistently-sized pieces for the group involved in the next stage of processing. Leftover pieces, called waste, are often used for fuel to heat the water boiler at the site, another stage in the process.

Rachael oversees all production issues, product design, packaging, research and development, and testing of possible new products.

Bambu designs, produces and markets housewares—more than 120 products—made from bamboo and cork, utilizing the materials in a different manner. The production process varies for many items, depending on the material and the product. There are eight collections: All Occasion Veneerware, Lacquerware, Serveware, Cutting and Serving Boards, Natural Utensils, Nesting Baskets, bambu KIDS and Cork Kitchen and Home.

Bambu designs, produces and markets housewares—120 products—made from bamboo and cork, utilizing the materials in a different manner.

A centuries old craft, "coiling" strips of bamboo to form bowls, trays and other serving pieces, is a process unique to Vietnam and "not replicated anywhere else," Jeff points out. Lacquering is a treatment usually applied to wood products, but here is used for bamboo laminates, specifically bowls, cutting boards and trays. He adds, "All bamboo products are cleaned with hot soapy water."

Bambu carries several lines of goods, including:

BAMBOO/VENEERWARE

- ≈ Plates—four sizes
- ≈ Eating utensils—adult fork, knife, spoon set
- ≈ Trays

LACQUERWARE/HAND-COILED BAMBOO

- ≈ Bowls—large, three colors
- ≈ Bowls—small, nine colors
- ≈ Bowls—mini, nine colors
- ≈ Bowls—low, five colors
- ≈ Bowls—kids, set of four colors

BAMBOO UTENSILS

- ≈ Eating—adult fork, knife, spoon set
- ≈ Eating—kids fork & spoon set
- ≈ Eating—babies fork and spoon set
- ≈ Eating—kids fork, knife, spoon set
- ≈ Eating—kids sporks (combination fork/spoon)
- ≈ Eating—kids chopsticks
- ≈ Cooking—spatulas
- ≈ Cooking—five types of spoons
- ≈ Cooking—five kinds of spatulas
- ≈ Cooking—mixing spoons, four sizes
- ≈ Kitchen fork
- ≈ Sporks—small, set of four
- ≈ Servers—oval salad servers, 12 inches
- ≈ Servers—set of two, available in four colors, 11 inches
- ≈ Servers—set of two, fork, spoon

- Kids in the Kitchen—set of five cooking utensils
- Spreaders
- Utensil holder
- Pot scrubber

STAINLESS AND BAMBOO
- Cheese Knife
- Cheese Planes
- Bread Knife
- Spreader

BAMBOO SERVING PIECES
- Bowl—salad
- Bowl—small salad
- Cups—condiment, two sizes
- Tray—large, 20 inches
- Trays—natural and three colors
- Trays—appetizer, three sizes
- Trays—oval, three sizes
- Double and triple dip
- Coasters

BAMBOO CUTTING & SERVING BOARDS
- Boards—three small sizes, two colors
- Boards—one shape, four sizes, one color
- Boards—crumb, plank, round, chop-scoop-serve
- Chopping Block

CORK ITEMS
- Bowls—three sizes
- Trays—appetizer, two sizes

    ⅈ Boards—cutting, three sizes

BASKETS

    ⅈ Nesting—round, set of three, four colors and multi

    ⅈ Nesting—oval, set of three, multi and natural colors

The team of carpenters and woodworkers in central China that manufacture cutting and serving pieces are formed as a cooperative and set their own prices based upon level of difficulty, material requirements, and time required. The team of basket weavers employed by bambu lives in a specific village in central Vietnam. They work directly with the village, which allows them to pay higher wages and eliminates a layer. In the supply chain and the production center where Veneerware is manufactured is a small-scale factory employing 30-40 local staff. As a result, bambu need not work with brokers or trading agents but directly with producers.

Bambu Kids is comprised of two different parts: bamboo feeding utensils made from single pieces of the non-chemical material without adhesives (certified organic) and sets of small sized cooking utensils called Kids in the Kitchen.

A new material for bambu, cork, launched its first cork collection—kitchen and home items—in early 2009. Cork is derived from the bark of Chinese oak trees and can be harvested eight to 10 times during its lifespan without damage to the trees.

Two new products, also introduced in 2009, are made from bamboo waste—the pieces not used in the cutting boards and trays production process, nor as a source for fuel —are named Bamboo Pebbles, a collection of 13 rounded shapes used for display and Bamboo Pebble Candles.

"We have had our source of bamboo Certified Organic by the International Certification Organization IMO (Institute for Marketecology) of Switzerland," Jeff explains. "We have had the material that is grown and harvested for our All Occasion Veneerware, Natural Utensils, and bambu Kids lines certified." Bambu hired IMO to conduct Fair Trade Audits of several of their partners' manufacturing operations because it is important to the owners that they work with groups who respect the fair trade principles.

Shipping materials are biodegradable or made from recycled content and all their packaging is Forest Stewardship Council (FSC)-certified paper or recycled materials. One of the shipping uncertainties bambu faces is weather, which can affect transportation and material.

According to Jeff, "currency fluctuation is an ongoing challenge." He is responsible for strategy, branding and marketing, international business development, legal issues, receiving orders, answering inquiries, processing and shipping products, overseeing human resources in China and Vietnam, sales management and technical information.

Bambu is managed from New York, which requires Rachael and Jeff to travel to the United States once or twice a year for trade shows and meetings with their New York team consisting of three full- and two part-time employees. Bambu employs 60 independent sales representatives, who contact retailers within their territories. They are responsible for sales and customer service operations and duties. Many bambu clients are located on the East Coast, as are warehouse facilities (in New Jersey).

Trade shows are a very important marketing tool for them, and the partners plan their U.S. trips to coincide with their important New York and European trade shows: International Housewares Show, New York International Gift Fair, Natural Products Expo, Catersource and Ambiente in Frankfurt. To find out how important a factor trade shows might be, in 2003 bambu tested its product offerings at key shows and were amazed by the results. They have since known that trade shows are indispensable for meeting prospective and existing customers who can touch and feel products and provide feedback as well as generate new business. In fact, industry shows represent a sizeable part of their marketing budget.

Giving back to the community is as important to the partners as the principles of fair trade. In China, bambu has provided furniture, books and gym equipment to a rural school that their workers' children attend. In Vietnam, they invested in an improved wastewater management solution in the village center, where a group of their weavers live. Because the workers are direct employees, they can be paid higher wages. Weaving supplements their farming income during non-harvest months.

In villages elsewhere in Vietnam, the partners are exploring ways to help physically disabled people, providing wheelchairs and other means to attain mobility, which translates into more jobs and self-support.

Rachael and Jeff also work with the Grameen Foundation (www.grameenfoundation.org) in China that provides micro-finance assistance around the world. They are members of the aptly named *1% for the Planet* wherein members contribute one percent of net sales toward the preservation and restoration of the natural environment. (www.onepercentfortheplanet.org)

Asked about plans for the immediate future, Jeff foresees using a new material—coconut—to produce a new product: a set of bowls made from normally discarded shells (waste); the first of many products to come.

∽

In addition to bambu, Rachel, Jeff, and partner Trine Targett own a retail shop called Nest. All three make China their home and work directly with the craftspeople and artisans in China and Asia who produce their goods from renewable or recycled materials. Together with their brand partners, Nest adheres to the same three tenets that define bambu: they are accountable for the processes they employ; they work to minimize waste; they support the communities in which they operate.

Nest occupies an enclosed glass-fronted 1,000 square foot loft space on the second floor of the International Artist Factory. A former candy factory, this original building now is the centerpiece of the thriving arts and shopping Taikang Lu district. Green spaces with park benches are beginning to mushroom around the factory, and the area is sprouting ultra-modern new shops.

Nest is in a former candy factory now the centerpiece of the thriving arts and shopping Taikang Lu district.

The district itself is one of the first mixed residential/retail areas in Shanghai. As a group of young companies engaged in expanding their product lines with Nest, the words 'fashionable and unusual' can truthfully apply to all. In addition to the products of bambu, they offer:

- décor and fashionable accessories
- natural fiber baby clothes
- classic women's clothing
- sustainable furniture with novel approaches
- fine bone china from Asia
- recycled bags and accessories
- handwoven Tibetan carpets
- reversible and recycled gift papers
- tags and note cards
- silk throws and pillows

- organic cotton bedding—70 percent bamboo/30 percent organic cotton—in many colors

- indigo dye accessories for men, women and children

- scrapped leather purses

Nest is comprised of small shops-within-a-shop, each area arranged with intriguing displays. The overall effect is a light-filled, airy, spacious environment. Nest designers hold designer talks and learning events in the shop. They share their processes, their goals, as well as stories of social enterprises such as Hands On China. This unique marketing idea is well-received by customers and others. Nest partners also give back. One partner supports a women's cooperative employing women in southwestern China. Another Nest partner, an interior design company, shares its research and environmental materials database to all people.

What is Jeff's advice to start-ups, whether it's wholesale, brick-and-mortar or Internet?

- Get others to believe in you

- Find ambassadors: people who are excited about what you do and are eager and willing to tell others

- Keep an eye on finances but don't let it be your guiding force

- Attend to details

- Everything matters: What you do. How you do it. Whom you involve. How you move it. How, what, when, where and why you talk about your business.

bambu
rachels@bambuhome.com
bambuhome.com
twitter: @bambuhome
284 Anfu Road, 2/f
Shanghai, China
Phone: (86-21) 5403-6814
Fax: (86-21) 5403-4714

Nest
International Artist Factor
Taikang Road, Lane 210
Studio 201 (2nd floor)
Shanghai, China
Phone: (86 21) 6466 9524
info@nestshanghai.com
nestshanghai.com

CHAPTER 3

FAIR TRADE

The concept of Fair Trade has been in development for at least 50 years, but only within the past 10 years have great strides been made to bring together different factions into an organized form of trade on a global scale to standardize regulation, labeling and certification.

Fair Trade's goal is to address the problem of marginalized men, women and children—individuals or entire communities—in Third World and developing countries who seek economic self-sufficiency. By using skills and craftwork that have been either indigenous to their area for centuries or can be taught, these impoverished communities can create products, sell them, and use the income to improve education, food supplies, sanitation, transportation, communication and— for many—chances of survival.

A local group wanting Fair Trade certification can contact any national Fair Trade association or organization. In turn, a Fair Trade group member visits the community, identifies its skills, designs and develops products requiring those skills, prices production of each item and ultimately gains Fair Trade certification for the new group. It then markets the products to small or large companies that, in turn, sell to world markets (generally through the Internet).

There are now thousands of Fair Trade items on the market—among them food and coffee, clothing and accessories, toys and jewelry—providing consumers with artisan-quality block printing, pottery-making, intricate leatherwork, exquisite hand embroidery, weaving, and tie-dying. The eco-friendly items usually incorporate local sustainable materials, including wood, cloth, tree bark, clay, organic minerals, flowers and seeds, among others.

According to Dastkar, a Fair Trade organization in Rajasthan, India, "A consumer does not buy out of compassion," meaning that products must have value and appeal. Indeed, consumers show appreciation for Fair Trade artisans.

Dastkar believes craftwork to be a "social, cultural and economic force that has enormous strength and potential within the economic mainstream of India." Dastkar ensures that the product is competitive in cost and aesthetic in feeling. One of its objectives is to teach people "the process of developing a craft," which includes skills training; design and product development; tailoring, cutting and sizing workshops; indigo and natural dying; firing and glazing (techniques for potters); costing; pricing; and credit, resulting in independence from commercial middlemen.

Millions of men, women, and children in many countries yearn for what most would consider basics: a home in a safe environment, the dignity of earning an income, safe food and water, and protection from unfair labor practices. An estimated 1.4 billion people around the world live on less than $1.25 per day, according to Bread for the World (www.bread.org). Many are forced into sweatshops and prostitution to survive. Fair Trade addresses these issues and more.

For the latest information on Fair Trade, including figures on global sales, beneficiaries, history, labeling and the certification process, the following websites provide links to dozens of related sites, or, since the Fair Trade world is expanding so rapidly, simply type "Fair Trade" into an Internet search engine.

    ⋞ www.fairtrade.net—Fairtrade International (FLO) is a global organization working to secure a better deal for farmers and workers by setting standards, facilitating business, and promoting trade justice.

ᐳ www.flo-cert.net—FLO-CERT GmbH is an international certification body. FLO and FLO-CERT split from the once single-body Fairtrade Labelling Organizations International.

ᐳ www.fairtradefederation.org—Fair Trade Federation consists of U.S. and Canadian Fair Trade retailers, wholesalers and importers. The website links to Fair Trade producer groups, acts as a clearinghouse for Fair Trade information and provides resources and networking opportunities to members.

ᐳ www.wfto.com—World Fair Trade Organization is a global organization of Fair Trade producer cooperatives and associations, export marketing companies, importers, retailers, and national and regional Fair Trade networks and support organizations. It launched the FTO Mark in 2004.

ᐳ www.wto.org—World Trade Organization provides a wealth of information about imports, exports, tariffs, and trade regulations.

EARTHTRIBE

Manita Senn, born and raised in India, owns the eco-conscious Internet business Earthtribe, based in Melbourne, Australia. Her deep interest in textiles and colors led her to college in Australia. When her daughter began school in 2007, Manita started her business, combining her interests in design, community groups, women, and India as well as her strong desire for children "to grow up understanding the importance of being involved and sharing the green world in which they all live." At the start, Manita's plan was to finance the business with a small capital outlay and to continually reinvest her profits, which has proved successful.

For several years, Manita has worked with organizations that have trading partners in India and around the world, and act on behalf of individual nomadic tribes belonging to larger community groups. These communities live close to the land and observe their own rules and regulations. Manita has access to about 12 such groups for different types of products. When she needs to order a particular item, she contacts via Internet the community group representing the tribe that creates the items. She deals with about 70 different products: 75 percent children's items and 25 percent housewares, such as cushion covers, hand-embroidered quilts and books, journals, gift wrappings, and elaborately decorated paper bags. Manita has handled as many as 100 products at times, and expects to again, depending on the tribes' output. She is beginning to explore the same type of operations in Sri Lanka and Laos.

Earthtribe's range of hand-lacquered products is sourced from community groups based in Channapatna, South India.

NS Toys are hand-lacquered wood products. The wood comes from local sustainable trees, and the bright colors from the bark, flowers and seeds of local plants. The 120 women who make the toys live in close proximity to each other in southern India. They belong to a community group managed by All India Artisans and Craftworkers Welfare Association. The toys Manita buys from them include bird whistles, stacking rings, rattles, key rings, Pull-Along Snail, maracas, and spinning tops. "Because the materials are 100 percent natural, they are completely safe," Manita explains, "a big selling point, especially for an online business."

An abacus of smooth, colorful wooden beads on sturdy metal pipes makes learning numbers, colors and sequencing fun.

Dastkar Ranthambore, whose members live in villages around Ranthambore Tiger Reserve in Rajasthan, helps women create a range of craft products with a Tiger motif—which emphasizes their concerns with the tiger and the surrounding forest.

Kala Raksha, a not-for-profit organization, consists of nomadic tribes in a desert area of India. Rabaris and Garasia Jats create complex styles of embroidery on fabric, some with tiny mirrors sewn in. Both groups use their techniques to make other products, such as stuffed toys, bags and purses, games, cushion covers and bedspreads. They are considered master craftswomen. Their embroidery styles require excellent eyesight. As a result of their work, many tribal women are unable to see well by middle age. Thus, patchwork and appliqué traditions—larger and less intricate—have surfaced because they are easier on the eyes. The fabric, among other uses, can be superimposed on the covers of journals, diaries and notebooks.

Borong Polok Handmade Paper Unit, a community-based group in nearby Sikkim, produces the paper for these products from the local Argali Plant. It undergoes a tie-dye process to make colorful and intricate patterns for carry bags.

The nonprofit Sadhna organization in Rajasthan brings together 380 women artisans to create a range of accessories like scarves, purses and housewares, such as hand-embroidered and patchwork silk throw pillows and bedspreads, by assisting with production and marketing. Artisans earn a fair share of their products' proceeds and also share the overall annual profit.

Through Fair Trade with the tribes, Earthtribe assists with the preservation of traditional crafts and skills that would otherwise be lost. In 2008, for example, some of Kala Raksha's artisans visited Melbourne where Manita organized an exhibition for them to speak about their work and showcase and sell their products.

Earthtribe also sources products from larger organizations, including Asha Handicrafts, Self-Employed Women's Association and South India Producer's Association—all internationally recognized Fair Trade organizations that give marketing support to groups of small producers and craftsmen cooperatives. They arrange healthcare and education programs and help connect them to commercial markets.

The wholesale division of Manita's business involves visiting each organization from which she sources products. She must first understand how each item works. Next she contacts a person in the organization with whom she can follow up on an order, which she typically places online after an initial small-quantity order. This "sampling" order consists of items produced in different styles and colors. Then she sends at least 40 percent of the total payment via PayPal and

Direct Electronic Banking. She pays on completion of the order. Often minimum quantities are required for production, varying between 25 to 100 pieces depending on the complexity of the production process for a particular item. Most items take at least eight weeks in production. So Manita must plan months ahead—design, production, quality checks, and shipping—to receive Earthtribe's shipment by her target date.

A new venture for Earthtribe is adding recycled and upcycled goods. New to her inventory are paper products: notebooks, pads, letter packs and journals. The paper pulp is produced from wood-free wastes such as cotton cuttings, leftover seed hairs culled from cotton balls (during the ginning process of turning the balls into thread) and the fibrous element of cotton seeds.

In place of brown paper bags are newspaper bags which are created from layers of newspaper. Karm Marg, an organization in New Delhi, collects discarded newspapers to make supermarket-type shopping bags. Profits from sales of these and other products —such as wastepaper baskets created from rice and cement sacks—provide income for street children. Candy wrappers are made into larger sheets, folded and woven, and transformed into cosmetic bags, handbags and clutch purses.

Markets and trade fairs are an important part of Manita's business. "Marketing is one of the most important components of a business," she says. "You can have the most innovative product but if it isn't visible and marketed properly, it will be lost. Finding the right marketing mix can be difficult and it's something that needs ongoing attention."

She participates in boutique, Christmas, and outdoor markets as well as in the important Organic and Eco Living expos. Her most important event is the National Fair Trade in May (part of Fair Trade Fortnight celebrations). "It provides the opportunity to speak with and learn from my consumers directly," she says. "Understanding your target market and changing trends is crucial. It's also a great way to present products to people in a real way, as the touch-and-feel of products is important." This is a particularly important factor for an Internet business because customers cannot touch or feel products.

Manita plans to participate in the Perth, Brisbane and Sydney gift fairs and a few trade shows in coming years. She makes "invaluable contacts" through these types of events and continues to marvel at the generosity and integrity of people in the Fair Trade industry.

In addition to trade shows, Manita's marketing program includes advertising and public relations. Her focus on marketing is exceptional, and she was gracious enough to pass on her most productive marketing tips:

- Manita lists Earthtribe in as many online directories as possible for maximum exposure.

- Earthtribe engages Google Adwords (paid online advertising) from time to time and is working on a Search Engine Optimization to reach more prospective customers.

- A few weeks before any big event, she prepares flyers and postcards for circulation and sends out a media release. She prepares an online campaign a few weeks prior to, and then again a few days prior to, the event, alerting customers to special events and activities.

- At most events, she surveys consumers to stay in tune with their needs, and uses that data to enhance her customer database. "I have found it very important to engage in public discussion and one-on-one conversations with people to understand trends, consumer frustrations and expectations," she advises. "Surveys also help us target our marketing to effectively reach different demographics.

🍃 Leading magazines have featured Earthtribe—the best (and least expensive) form of marketing. She also advertises in leading parenting magazines, but finds print advertising too expensive for the return.

🍃 Through its website, Earthtribe sends newsletters to its customer base to promote latest news, new products, upcoming events and specials.

🍃 Manita is setting up a social media presence through Twitter and Facebook, and publishes a handsome blog.

Manita shares a success story:

"A month or so after I launched the business, I sat down and wrote an article on Earthtribe and its conception. I was still working out my marketing strategy and was unsure how to explore the different options. I sent a draft of an article to a few leading magazines that had a good circulation around Melbourne, and included photos of some of our products. To my utter surprise, I had a couple of responses, and before I knew it, I was being interviewed. A few weeks later a two-page article appeared in a magazine that is distributed free to households in and around Melbourne. What followed was beyond my expectation. I had businesses approach me to stock my products and the online sales zoomed up. The exposure I received was a fantastic start to my new business. To this day, I wonder where the business would have been if not for that article. It gave me and the business one of the biggest boosts yet!"

She has since learned to take chances and try a variety of marketing ideas and media, print and online.

People often ask Manita how Earthtribe came about. Her response, "The driving force has always been to do the right thing by the people who make these wonderful products; to keep traditional art forms alive; to empower women who are marginalized; and to use raw materials that do not exploit the environment. It just makes good sense and is fair to all involved."

Earthtribe
Phone: 0 410 619 746 (within Australia)
Phone: +61 410 619 746 (from overseas)
earthtribes.blogspot.com
manita@earthtribe.com.au
www.earthtribe.com.au

CARINI LANG

Joe Carini is, first and foremost, an artist. He belongs to that rarified world of perfectionists who attend to every little detail and take a gut-wrenching approach to producing their babies—and in Joe's case, his "babies" are exquisite, eco-friendly custom carpets and rugs. This is how I "felt" Joe rather than saw him, perhaps because of his palpable passion and unusual pride in his art. For Joe, the creative process is personal.

From 1979 to 1982, Joe studied drawing, painting and sculpture. He then studied at the National Academy for two years and art history at Hunter College and the Art Students League. In the late 1980s, he studied art on his own for a year in Italy, developing his personal aesthetic. For six years he sold carpets and textiles in New York, where he found unusual antique carpets to sell to elite collectors and dealers. By that time, he was considered a "picker," working for someone else. He became "infatuated" with antique carpets and went to Nepal to study colors, specialized natural dyes, designs and carpet-weaving techniques.

Joe first visited Nepal in 1992, after learning that the country had excellent natural raw materials. He traveled back and forth, establishing specific techniques for dyeing and production through constant experimentation. Perhaps because he had Tibetan friends, many of his carpets reflect intricate Tibetan techniques and heritage. Joe created a vast range of natural handmade rugs in Nepal and sold to renowned interior designers, architects and private collectors worldwide.

In 1998, he and his partner, Aurelie Lang, who has a business administration and finance background, opened their own showroom, Carini Lang, in the Tribeca neighborhood of New York City. Aurelie was the driving force in organizing and developing the company and now oversees administration, public relations and marketing. Their team consists of six full-time and three part-timer employees.

To finance their launch, the couple used only personal funds, avoiding credit. Their public relations programs bring customers into their showroom. The two most effective programs have been open houses and speaking engagements. Since opening, Carini Lang earned laudatory articles in many magazines, including The New York Times Magazine, Elle Décor, Metropolitan Home, and House Beautiful.

In 2008, Amy Redford (daughter of Robert Redford) debuted her first film, The Guitar, about a young woman with a short time to live who moves to an expensive Manhattan loft and surrounds herself with only the most beautiful, one-of-a-kind furnishings. The choice of a rug: Carini Lang.

For any new business, having insiders write about the company and filmmakers prominently show products is not only a compliment, but also the most valuable form of advertising that money cannot buy.

Carini Lang offers four design themes, all from Nepal, and most 100 percent green and hand-woven using silk, wool, nettle, hemp and cashmere. Hemp has a history of use as carpet backing; the fiber is strong, rot-resistant qualities and nontoxic fumes in case of a fire.

Categories include Animal Prints, Contemporary, Florals and Textures, with inspirations such as Fish Skin and Tiger (in various color combinations), Corduroy Silk, ultra-contemporary Scratchout Plaid, Italian Flower Garden, and Tibetan and Indian themes. Customers often request a particular design in customized colors.

The only paid marketing—and by far the most effective, according to Joe—is magazine advertising in publications such as Interior Design and Architectural Digest.

They conduct all business in the showroom/retail store. Because of the nature of the business—custom, one-of-a-kind carpets and rugs—Carini Lang has a website, but does not sell via e-commerce Joe's goal is to have more patron clients who will commission rarified carpets and rugs.

About 80 percent of Carini Lang stock is green, and rises well-above commercially produced carpets. Joe's definition of green consists of three core principles. The product must:

- benefit the workers who weave the rugs

- protect the environment during production

- be a unique work of art using 100 percent natural materials.

- Moreover, the company uses sustainable, chemical-free resources to protect the environment, and it pays good wages and uses no child or forced labor.

The process of creating a Carini Lang carpet is fascinating, especially because of Joe's technique. He developed most of the colors by working in dye houses for extended periods, learning from different masters. He always visualized the palette he wished to achieve, colors not found in anyone's existing palettes. By "an effort of will and determination" and many years of experimentation, Joe has almost achieved his long-cherished dream.

The dyes that produce the colors come from indigo, madder and many varieties of flowering plants, plus fruit and nut trees, in addition to the bark or wood of sustainable trees, vines and roots. Some plants are considered sacred because Ayurvedic medicines, having special healing properties, come from them. Therefore, medicine markets in Nepal buy the dyes from these plants. Parts from the bark, wood, vines, roots, flowers, fruit and nuts have certain properties that designate whether they are crushed or ground. They heat to a low boil in vats. Some dyes need natural mordants, usually iron salt or alum, which act as binding agents. These, too, affect the colors. The final color is the result of how the raw materials are treated.

After a carpet is woven on a loom, it goes to the washing area, where it is submerged and soaked in a pool of clean water. Then the carpet is laid flat on a concrete platform for soaping. The soap is hand-made from a small fruit that forms a hard skin when dried; it is this skin that produces the fruit soap. The soap gives a fresh, natural wash compared to carpets washed with chemicals and caustics. After lathering the carpet is carefully rinsed. A squeegee is used to eliminate as much water as possible. The carpet is stretched on a trampoline-like frame and left to dry in the sun. When dry, it is taken to a shearing room to ensure an even surface. Finally it is hand sew, bound and fringed.

Natural fibers and dyes create carpets and rugs that are comfortable, durable works of art using processes that protect the environment.

In the final step, the carpet is inspected before being packed and shipped by air to New York to satisfy the "instant gratification demands of our clients," Joe says. They hope to change the shipping method and reduce the carbon footprint, but they would probably lose too much business if they made the change hastily. "My clients are very demanding and not used to waiting for anything," Joe explains.

Carini Lang is a longtime member of Green America and Good-Weave (formerly RugMark International) because of the organizations' commitment these goals:

- deterrence of child labor
- education and rehabilitation of rescued child workers in the carpet industry
- service to the families and communities of more than 3,200 children in Nepal and India

Long before it was popular, Carini Lang was recycling paper and employing eco-friendly methods in the office and showroom. The company purchases all products through Green America (www.greenamerica.org). Carini Lang belongs to Green America, whose publication, The National Green Pages, bills itself as "the only nationwide directory of socially and environmentally responsible businesses coast-to-coast." The organization—which represents a niche for architects, designers and manufacturers—sponsors green festivals in San Francisco and Washington, D.C.

Approximately 20 percent of showroom carpets are special orders by clients "who want what they want," Joe concedes. That means a small percentage of rugs fall short of the 100 percent natural mark. Joe will try to change clients' minds about materials or dyes that are not eco-friendly, but they usually remain firm on their choices.

Joe is determined to eventually make only all-natural rugs. "How can a carpet be beautiful if the process of making it was destructive and negative [not 100 percent natural]?" he wonders.

Carini Lang
335 Greenwich St.
New York, NY 10013
Phone: (646) 613-0497
info@carinilang.com
www.carinilang.com

CHAPTER 4

SETTING UP AN INTERNET BUSINESS

The first rule in the Primary Principles of Retailing applies as much to an online store as it does to an on-site store: "The Right Item, at the Right Price, in the Right Place at the Right Time."

Businesses today must set up a website to help maximize exposure to consumers. Starting an online business has many steps in common with the brick-and-mortar approach. The biggest difference between the two is the competition: a retail shop located on a lovely street in town might have no neighborhood competition. But as an online business, that same store competes with hundreds, if not thousands of websites selling similar goods at similar prices from around the world. Consumers find the competition with only a few mouse clicks.

A fundamental knowledge of both business and the Internet are essential to an effective website. An inexpensive and simple way to acquire this foundation is through Service Corps of Retired Executives, or SCORE, a resource partner of the U.S. Small Business Administration.

Whether on-site or online, a business plan comes first. For a bank loan, raising money, comparison of actual performance and initial projections, and identifying of omissions and flaws in your overall concept, the business plan is absolutely necessary.

Most new entrepreneurs don't know where to start when creating a business plan. That's why SCORE's free service is most helpful. Score (www.score.org) provides a gallery of downloadable "Templates & Tools" essential to new business entrepreneurs, including:

BUSINESS PLANNING TEMPLATES

- Business Plan for a Start-up Business
- Business Plan for an Established Business
- Competitive Analysis

FINANCE TEMPLATES

- Start-Up Expenses
- Opening Day & Projected Balance Sheets
- Bank Loan Request for Small Business
- Breakeven Analysis
- Cash Flow Statement (12 Month & 3 Year)
- Financial History & Ratios
- Personal Financial Statement
- Profit and Loss Projection (12 Month & 3 Year)

SALES TEMPLATE

- Sales Forecast (12 Months)

Adapted from www.score.org. Special thanks to the Seattle SCORE Chapter for developing these user-friendly planning templates. (http://seattle.score.org)

A plan includes a description of the business, merchandise, marketing and sales strategies. Detailed financial projections, such as income and expenses itemized by categories, including a projected cash flow statement, both for 24 months, should be included in the plan. A summary of goals and objectives, an overview with the business description, and a paragraph explaining how you expect to succeed rounds out the plan. This information will be required by those with the potential to offer funding and other assistance. What's more, the business owner benefits by thinking through every aspect of the business to reveal its strengths, weaknesses and feasibility. It provides an opportunity to overcome the weaknesses before actually opening for business. This can make all the difference between long-term success and short-term failure.

As for securing a loan, in addition to your own funds, and perhaps those of relatives and friends, SCORE suggests one or more partners who would act as underwriters. SBA loan programs, credit unions, or local banks—preferably in your neighborhood and therefore having an elevated interest in your business success—are also possibilities.

Steps to set up your wholesale/retail business on the Internet, build a website, and manage an online business are preceded by the most important factor you need to know: it can take up to a year from preliminary research to actual start-up. Therefore, begin preliminary research with as much lead time as possible.

Begin with the obvious question: Does a potential market exist for your business, product(s), or idea? Be sure it is a niche business or product, and specialize in it, which is the road to success in today's market. A 'niche' means a specific market segment in which you can distinguish your business through originality in product differentiation and a nimble approach to serving and growing a well-defined target audience.

Second, follow up with a comparison of existing online businesses. Are they basically the same products or does one stand out as unique? Take teddy bears, for example. If a business carries plush teddy bear pillows, teddy bear toys, and a tiny teddy key chain, and you see them on other sites, you probably would not want to compete with that line or business, nor would it be considered a niche, in this instance. If, however, your teddy bears are clay cookie jars, pottery bear plant pots, baking dishes, kitchen utensil holders, painted wood mailboxes, and toy chests, this theme could well constitute a niche operation—original and/or perhaps nonexistent elsewhere online.

Thousands of small businesses fail every year due to under-funding, under-planning or because they sold products similar to companies that have a large market share.

Third, explore how to find your potential customer base online. Before you start looking, list the types of customers you want. Are they shopping for themselves, for family members, or for gifts? What are they willing to pay for similar products? Learn what your potential customers want, what your competitors are selling, and at what prices. Then analyze how much time and finances you have to allocate to your web business.

Several agencies provide free guidance covering the more complex rules and regulations for online sales. SBA's free Online E-Commerce Course teaches how to build a website and manage an online business.

An online business also has legal and financial considerations, particularly in areas of privacy and security, and possibly copyright and taxation. Laws covering digital rights and online advertising may also apply, and these could include e-commerce rules and regulations; collecting sales tax over the Internet; international selling/exporting.

The www.business.gov website "helps small businesses understand their legal requirements and locate government services supporting the small business community." In addition, eHow offers a step-by-step guide "How to Set Up an Online Business" at www.ehow.com.

The Federal Trade Commission is the primary federal agency regulating e-commerce, including use of commercial emails, consumer privacy and online advertising. FTC's e-Commerce Guide provides an overview of its rules and regulations, and you can communicate with a representative of the FTC via e-mail or telephone.

It is important to research the rules and regulations before creating your website, because that research might need to be incorporated into your web pages. After doing your homework then design your website. You need Internet access and website building tools to accomplish this, and there are myriad Internet sources offering free advice and design tools for designing a website.

Whichever you choose, there are a few basic steps to planning your site.

Begin by securing a domain name; this will provide you with a URL (Uniform Resource Locator). This is your Internet address and identity. There are different kinds of domain name extensions, but "dot com" (.com) is by far the most common and easiest for the consumer to remember. Do a thorough Internet search, read articles and books relating to domain name selection. Take the advice of professionals. Do not allow your haste to force you into an obscure or difficult-to-remember domain name. Avoid cryptic, or overly-clever names that amuse you, but might confuse the consumer.

Ideally, your company name and its domain name should be identical. Try some potential misspellings of your domain name to rule out the very real possibility that you could inadvertently send business to a competitor or, perhaps worse, to a website with embarrassing content. Also check other file extensions (.net, .org, .biz, etc.) to see what happens if your customer were to make that common error. Examine your URL carefully in its simplest form—no spaces, all lower case—to see if the order of letters can be read another way. Visit one of the many websites or blogs that have compiled lists of the more 'unfortunate' domain names to see some humorous, and horrifying, examples of this.

Hundreds of companies host domain names (web hosts), often competitively priced, so narrow your search to a secure and reliable host/service provider with the features you will need. Read user reviews as well as reviews from independent researchers and computer journals. Websites are not one-size-fits-all, nor will your company stay one size. Plan ahead for the inevitable: change.

Choose and list your products for your online e-commerce store, preferably these will be niche/specialty products and variations. In some cases it will not be feasible for every item you sell in your on-site retail store to be sold in your online store. For example, a pet store may sell kitten food and kitten toys online, but not the kittens themselves. They could be featured on the website, however. Your 'kitten of the week' photo, video or web cam could attract cat lovers who are very likely to be cat owners and future customers.

If you are not using pre-designed templates provided by your domain host, but are designing your site from scratch, you can use software such as Template Builder or Dreamweaver to start this process. Before doing this, ask yourself, "Am I a store owner or a web designer?" If you are not a web designer, it is recommended you not design your own web pages.

Your template, or web designer, will create a banner, a content area, and navigation menus—a directory of your site pages that appears on each page allowing customers to comfortably navigate your site. Visit websites of your competitors. Decide if you want to blend in or stand out; there may be a clear benefit to one or the other. Web design professionals can emulate other sites. Find one you like and design your site with a similar look and feel taking care not to infringe anyone's copyright.

Add quality photos of your products for potential customers to view. Most web building tools include an option that allows the customer to click on a photo to get more information about the product specifications and price. Perhaps not literally, but it can be said a photo is worth a thousand clicks.

Secure shopping cart services encourage customers to buy your products with ease. 'Buy Now' and 'Add to Cart' buttons, for example, automate the purchase by steering customers directly to a secure payment system where they will be given a choice: usually credit/debit card, but often a payment transfer service such as PayPal. The order page also provides essential tax and shipping information and reiterates your return policy.

Shopping cart services will be necessary for true e-commerce. Investigate the service providers, read the reviews, and choose your own, or trust your web designer to choose one for you. As an inexpensive but less desirable alternative, you can sell products from your website by taking orders over the phone or via e-mail or fax.

Consider the option of an electronic fax service, such as eFax, for customers who do not have e-mail, or who are 'uncomfortable' with e-commerce. Faxes are received via e-mail. Your reply can be sent via return fax, or back through the electronic fax service. You may not need a conventional fax machine at all if you have a printer/scanner.

It is essential to promote your website widely. For optimum results, consider paying search engines that offer enhanced search results and preferred placement. You or your web designer should put effort into selecting the right search tags which are the essential keywords search engines use to find your site. Periodically search for yourself as if you were the customer, or ask a friend to find you online.

Take advantage of existing and emerging site-building tools. Business marketing is reaching into the social networking world. Hundreds of free-to-the-user social networks, such as Facebook and Twitter, exist worldwide. Blogging about a subject related to your niche product can drive traffic to your site. Joining social networks related to your products exposes that audience to your online store.

If your knowledge about a subject is sufficient, answer questions in forum sites. As a pet store owner you may have expertise in what to feed kittens. How fortuitous you also sell kitten food.

Establish policies for voiding orders, processing exchanges, issuing refunds, etc. Do this before start-up, and clearly state these policies on your website to avoid misunderstandings or complaints from your customers.

Be sure to include the capability to create and maintain a visitor or customer list. This will be a valuable future marketing resource you can use to send updates to your customers about new products and special offers.

Include an e-mail address for customers to contact you for more information; this can be as simple as info@[your-domain.com], which can be forwarded to your home or business e-mail address, or smartphone, so you see it right away. An auto-reply feature can alert the customer with a brief 'got your message' reply, with the promise you will reply in depth within a certain number of hours or days.

Long before you receive your first order, you should have compared prices and services of reliable shipping companies, such as UPS, FedEx and USPS, to ensure that your service offers online tracking, allowing both you and your customers to check delivery status.

There are hundreds of domain hosts that provide tools for setting up business websites, with or without using templates. The following are not specific recommendations, but examples: Yahoo! Small Business (smallbusiness.yahoo.com) has three plans that provide the tools to set up your store. For professional help there are sites, such as One Choice For Your Store (www.1choice4yourstore.com), that assist in building and maintaining your store.

Additional services to consider when choosing a domain host include an easy-to-use order-management system for processing and tracking; automatic fax or e-mail alerts on receipt of a new order; risk tools to help identify fraudulent orders; free or discounted promotional materials, such as business cards, brochures, flyers and post cards for handing out, including with orders, or mailing.

Shortly before your on-site grand opening or your online launch, send a press release announcing the news to editors at newspapers, magazines and websites that cover new businesses for general consumer and industry/trade audiences. Include facts about your niche, products you are carrying and other important information.

Your web address should appear on all promotional and advertising materials and e-mails, whether online or on paper. Always proofread the materials before they go to print and ask someone who has 'the power of knowing nothing' to see what information might be missing. You might be surprised to know how many grand openings have been advertised without key facts such as the date or the location. Always include the area code and full address, including zip code. Out of town visitors don't always know what area code they are in, and some mapping systems rely on zip code information.

Be accurate, complete and generous with information about how, when and where to find your business.

For some, setting up a website will be a breeze. For others, it might seem daunting. But rest assured, website templates are designed to be easy to use; online help and web design professionals are readily available. Take advantage of all resources, many of which are free.

The rewards of a successful online business are so great that it is business suicide in the 21st century to forgo creating one, especially if your established on-site business is struggling. One recently retired owner, whose business shrunk in his last several years, said he regretted not having a website and added he might otherwise still have been in business; he was only 58 and "not ready for retirement." Was he old-fashioned or stubborn? "Probably both," he concedes.

AUTONOMIE PROJECT

This is the story of a small business barely out of the start-up stage. It is an in-depth study of how to combine a distributorship/wholesale operation and online retail store. It is, in fact, almost a blueprint of a start-up, a green start-up.

Anne O'Loughlin is the founding partner and president of Autonomie Project, distributors of men's, women's and children's footwear, clothing and accessories, located in Boston. In addition to Anne and her co-partner/co-owner, Gina Williams, there are two other permanent members of the team, art director Mike Chevalier, and webmaster Michael Cuttita. To complete the team, two interns are recruited every college semester during summer or after graduation for work experience in the business field.

Autonomie Project (AP) is primarily a distributorship that offers up-to-the-minute stylish clothing and footwear that is also green. The two founding partners believed that fashion and Fair Trade could be incorporated into one. This was the challenge: items could not look like stereotypical eco-friendly clothing of yesteryear—to be blunt, frumpy. Rather, the products must be fashionable while also reflecting the values of the AP team's lifestyle—values each team member espouses: reduce waste, take part in one's community, use alternative forms of transportation, and as vegan/vegetarians, belong to local co-op markets.

The official definition of a distributor or wholesaler is "one who sells to retailer" but Autonomie Project wears other hats as well. As partners, they collaborate with their British partners on design and product development. As distributors, they buy products from a wholesaler who buys from a manufacturer. Also as distributors, they sell wholesale to retailers in the United States and Canada, in bulk. As retailers, they sell items directly to the consumer; in this case, from the company's on-line store.

The business has contracts with London-based companies whose products are exported from their manufacturers directly to AP's warehouse in the United States where items are, in turn, distributed to retailers large and small. When an American or Canadian retailer contacts Autonomie Project's British wholesale partner to place an order, the company automatically emails the order to AP, the exclusive North American distributor.

A start-up in December 2007, Autonomie Project became partners with British wholesaler, Fair Deal Trading, for their Ethletic footwear, a line of organic and Fair Trade sneakers and flip flops. The manufacturer, Talon Sports, is an independent company that owns and operates a factory in Pakistan, now certified by Fairtrade International (FLO), a workers' welfare fund. Talon manufactures an exclusive line of 100 percent organic cotton canvas sneakers for Autonomie Project. The canvas is from India while the certified green rubber used to make treaded soles, comes from Sri Lanka. The way cotton is woven makes it canvas; the way natural tree rubber is harvested makes it certifiable as "green".

Today the sneaker options consist of six styles of men's high tops in three colors; five styles of unisex low tops in four colors (including the latest, cranberry red) and six styles each of children's and youth low tops in several colors. Fair Trade cotton shoelaces come in six colors for a total of thirty-three items. In 2010 Autonomie Project launched adult wide sizes in two colors.

Another Ethletic product, flip flops, made entirely of rubber, is a Fair Trade product certified by the FSC and TransFair USA. They are manufactured in two colors (light blue with green soles and ocean blue with gray sole) and in unisex sizes for both adults and kids—all natural and 100 percent vegan. Each pair of flip-flops is enclosed in a 100 percent organic cotton reusable carrying bag.

A new silhouette, a slip-on/laceless model with different styles for men and for women is more a casual shoe than sneaker. More colors of sneakers, mandarin orange and navy, and two new styles of flip-flops are slated for next year.

The company has two major seasons a year: spring and fall—and a smaller holiday season. But because sneakers are a year-round product, Autonomie Project maintains high stock levels of all sizes and colors. All other products are seasonal therefore slated for sales twice a year, in January and August.

In 2009 the second partnership, Autonomie Project and Hug UK collaborated to produce a line of cute, quirky clothing items for babies, toddler and children called Little Green Radicals. The 100 percent Fair Trade organic cotton collection is made using biodynamic agriculture from Fair Trade-certified Egyptian cotton, the highest quality cotton known. Each item is stitched in a Fair Trade facility in India that employs 120 women who are handicapped or economically disadvantaged. The factory provides these women with jobs, training, food and accommodations.

'Little Green Radicals' is a model company that is not only providing high quality but also an opportunity to instill environmental and social justice in children." explains Ann—which sums up most of Autonomie Project's philosophy.

The collection of six items for children come in six colors (combination and solids) of pink and green, red and navy, orange and black, and solid white emblazoned with funky-colored stripes and funny sayings embroidered (dyes are certified organic) on the front. Styles offered include two one-piece bodysuits, two playsuits (short sleeves or ankle length) and bibs for babies, two tees (short and long sleeve) and two hoodies (pullovers) for toddlers and young children.

From a playsuit for babies ('Locally Produced') to both types of tees ('I Recycle My Tantrums', 'Get Up, Stand Up',

'Free Range', 'Keep the Planet Cool') the collection of mixed prints, colors and sayings is kids' world high style.

In 2010 Autonomie Project introduced a new combination of prints and other catchy phrases on the two tees and a pullover hoodie ('Give Peas a Chance'), two bibs ('Panda Monium'), ('Melting Hearts'); a one-piece bodysuit ('Smells Like Green Spirit'), an apple appliqué playsuit and two organic wool hug-me animals (Ivor the Pig and Ellie the Sheep) hand-knitted in Kenya with natural plant dyes by rural Kenyan women who utilize their knitting and spinning skills to support their families and improve their quality of life.

Baby's outfit is Little Green Radicals top and skirt, and Ethletic sneakers. Dad is wearing Autonomie Project's t-shirt and Ethletic sneakers.

Late in the year, the company introduced a new tee ('Stop the Wailing'), a little girls' line of two A-line dresses with mix and match leggings, skirt and 'panda' blouse.

The entire Little Green Radicals inventory consists of six styles of bibs, three styles of one-piece bodysuits, six playsuits, eight short-sleeve tees, seven long sleeve tees, three hoodies and two zip sweatshirts for a total of thirty-five items.

Sometimes a supplier will agree to manufacture a special product. In this case, Autonomie Project had enough demand for coordinated product colors that Hug UK and Fair Trade Dealing agreed to coordinate the colors of Ethletic children's sneakers with Little Green Radicals apparel so that not only do original designs and color schemes now coordinate with their new designs and color schemes but also with the footwear.

Future launchings include a new line of socks and arm/leg warmers made in the United States of regenerated or recycled cotton. This would be the only American company because all others with whom Autonomie Project has distribution agreement/contracts/partnerships are London-based; in fact, other than the one United States manufacturer, all others are located in India, Sri Lanka, Peru or Pakistan.

A new line of adult and children's underwear and sleepwear, Pants to Poverty, is in partnership with Autonomie Project and a new British Fair Trade wholesaler.

The company's private label t-shirt collection offers ten printed styles plus four colors for men and the same for women's for a total of eighteen items. One of the men's shirts is the 'Superhero Vegan' tee with the tag line 'Vegans Saving the World One Bite at a Time' and sales of this shirt raise funds for Farm Sanctuary, a non-profit animal shelter and anti-cruelty organization.

Autonomie Project gives 25 percent of each t-shirt purchase to Farm Sanctuary as one of their corporate sponsors. These adult shirts are United States made from a 35/65 poly-cotton fabric blend, with a green twist: the polyester is made from recycled soda bottles and the cotton is made from recycled cotton fabric scraps. AP also has a new 100 percent organic cotton t-shirt in the works that supports organic farming.

The company adheres to green practices religiously. They reuse all incoming shipping and mailing boxes and materials and only 100 percent post-consumer recycled materials for the company's mailing, printing, shipping and marketing. In addition, they print all their marketing materials and banners at local union shops using eco-friendly materials and techniques.

Team members practice the following principles, individually and in business:

- use products that are 100 percent vegan (including dyes, and the glue used in sneakers)
- donate to animal rights groups
- support legislation to end animal abuse
- company plants a tree with every purchase

Who purchases Autonomie Project products? They are in the 18-40-age range, highly educated, enjoy intellectual pursuits and share the company's values:

- Support local communities
- Support environmental issues
- Support human rights ("Fair Dealers")

These customers are idealistic individuals, passionate about other causes in their age range and more and more of them are having children.

While she was attending Tufts University, Anne O'Loughlin studied abroad in Venice and Madrid. Later she taught Spanish to young children in a small village in Spain. During her senior year at Tufts she was accepted into a program called Education for Public Inquiry and International Citizenship. While working with the Institute for Global Leadership she was asked to write a policy briefing for the Strategic Planning Unit of the Executive Office of the Secretary General of the United Nations on enforcing labor standards in East Asia in order to eradicate poverty.

She then won a grant to conduct research in Taiwan on the impact of the East Asian financial crisis on labor migration flows and the living and working conditions of Taiwanese migrant workers. Following that, she worked as federal investigator for the enforcement branch of HUD's Fair Housing Division. About that time, she connected with the founding team of a company (like AP) as their COO.

In 2007 she decided to start her own company.

In keeping with her principles Anne does not commute to an office. Her office is in her home. Team members live within walking distance of each other allowing them to work from home full time. Anne runs the company via email, teleconference, instant messaging and text messaging. The electricity and gas used in her home are provided by wind energy. All printing is done on recycled paper either in the office or at a local printer where anyone on the team can walk to the print shop to pick up orders.

∽

Co-owner Gina Williams' responsibilities involve mostly communications. Gina:

- manages and edits the company blog, including researching, scheduling and assigning topics to staff writers

- deals with inquiries and requests from press and bloggers concerning requests for interviews, and about products

- manages the company's presence on social network sites (MySpace, Facebook, Twitter)

- manages many wholesale accounts and helps with new retailer outreach, in particular feedback about what is selling and what is not—important facts for retailers who order less frequently

- assists with customer service and fulfillment of orders, wholesale, retail and inventory

> 🕭 prepares and manages booths for events, festivals and shows

> 🕭 manages Autonomie Project's band sponsorship exchange program (free Autonomie Project merchandise for bands' promotion of Autonomie Project.)

༺ঞ༻

Michael Cuttita is the webmaster and also a co-owner of Autonomie Project. He now owns his own business with Autonomie Project as a client. Michael lives and works in New York.

༺ঞ༻

Mike Chevalier is the company's art director. Mike is responsible for the development of Autonomie Project's brand, marketing materials, web design and overall aesthetics. He has plans to start up his own design firm with Autonomie Project as a client.

༺ঞ༻

Every semester the company recruits two college interns. They gain college credit, valuable work experience and a reference on their resumes. Derek Rogers works in the office part-time now and is a marketing major. Hannah Bybee attends the University of Utah where she is earning her MBA in marketing and finance and is working for Autonomie Project via email and videoconference.

Both interns are assigned a wide variety of projects, among them: gathering feedback from the retailers, suggesting improvements, displays they would like to see developed, and cold-calling prospective retailers. In addition, Derek has developed his own special project for Autonomie Project, a "home party" program where consumers can download marketing materials from the company website, order samples, and host their own "trunk shows" for friends, neighbors and family in their own homes—earning a discount on products they buy for themselves. Instructions are included on how to set up parties such as a baby shower that focuses on natural, Fair Trade items...in other words, green products.

As her special project, Hannah wrote a grant application for Autonomie Project and is working on an educational presentation about the company and its mission that can be downloaded from Autonomie Project's website for talks, seminars and presentations.

∽

Anne's position as CEO rounds out the picture of the team. Anne:

- is the point-of-contact who speaks at panels, seminars and events and the "face" of Autonomie Project

- networks and meets with other companies for potential partnerships

- is the "big picture" person who manages her team by identifying the task or goal that needs to be done and assigns tasks and deadlines

- creates all marketing materials, websites and communications (together with Mike and Michael) and that duty includes managing, guiding and critiquing the entire design process

- writes most of the copy for hang tags, t-shirt designs, the wholesale catalogue, press releases, website, and the company's e-newsletter

- organizes, casts and directs photo shoots

- manages the company's books—financial, insurance, and tax documents and filings

- deals with incoming requests from new retailers and fulfills current retailers orders

- reviews advertising offers and decides which ones to buy

- is responsible for day-to-day operations including answering emails and phone, managing the budget, buying all office supplies, hiring the cleaners and taking out the recycling and the trash!

Before starting up, Anne did not write a business plan, seek a loan or other outside investment; rather, she sought a partnership for her first product line with Fair Deal Trading's Ethletic footwear. They worked out a deal whereby Fair Deal Trading pre-financed all initial orders and billed Autonomie Project quarterly only for product sold during that period. It was essentially "on consignment." The rest of the original financing came from credit cards and personal savings accounts. To this day Anne and her partners still have no outside investors but continue to rely on terms from their business partners, like Hug UK, credit cards and personal funds. "We build our business solely off the sales we make," Anne explained.

Also before starting up, Anne attended Boston's natural Products Expo East and Down to Earth trade show as a visitor. Since 2008 Autonomie Project has had a booth, table, or some kind of presence at a great many festivals and fairs during festival season April to November. "The festivals usually have something to do with our three missions: environmentalism, Fair Trade, (cultural awareness, local art), or vegetarianism," Anne explained. The festivals range from musical concerts to eco expos such as the Green Festival in Seattle and San Francisco and the Eco Gift Festival in Santa Monica, California to food and art festivals along the East Coast many in Boston. Anne and members of the team personally sell their products at these events.

Sales from 2008-2009, Autonomie Project's first full year, were exactly on the nose at 150 percent, the projection for insurance purposes. The year 2009-2010 showed an increase of 60 percent growth in sales and 150 percent growth in net income. Figures for 2010-2011 are not yet known.

They also send out discount coupons about once a month, donations for silent auctions and products for display to a wide variety of events held around the country. They do not solicit these events; the event coordinators contact them requesting AP's information and displays.

Bloggers are a source of free non-trade publicity; they simply want to write about the company and/or review their products or they are hosting a give-away to which Autonomie Project donates a bonus for the readers. Another source of free publicity has been print articles or interviews that have appeared in Women's Wear Daily, Earnshaw's and Footwear News, and online publications like The Daily Green, Boston Phoenix, Change.org and the Los Angeles Times online.

Anne would very much like to appear as a participant at one of the large trade shows in New York or Boston but feels the company is still somewhat small in addition to not yet having the funding for such ventures—the shows are very expensive.

ঞ

The online store is where and how Autonomie Project sells their retail products directly to consumers. "These days it's almost an unwritten requirement for retail operations to have an online presence," declared Anne, "and the overhead is a lot less than a tradition shop/store operation." She explained that the company expends a lot of energy and money promoting the online store at the festivals, with partnerships, link exchanges, and coupon exchanges with other like-minded companies and organizations, as well as online directory listings, the company newsletter and social networks. They never stop looking for ways to boost online sales. Customers who shop their online store can pay with American Express, MasterCard, Visa, PayPal, or mail a check.

ঞ

Asked what her goal for Autonomie Project is in five years, Anne replied:

- ঞ To build (or be in) stores or shops with cafés

- ঞ To carry more areas of apparel and footwear

- ঞ To ultimately become a premier brand

- To have a shopping site of 50 percent distributor/50 percent retail

- To sell "niche" products of a mainstream green brand to mainstream consumers

∽

What advice does Anne have for new retailers regarding financing?

- If it is an on-site shop or store a Small Business Association (SBA) or local bank loan is necessary—in addition to personal funds.

- If it is a distributorship with online retail, negotiate for partnerships with your suppliers.

"One of the things I love most about small start-up enterprise," Anne conveys, "is that the work environment is so intense, pressure-filled, time-consuming and exciting it creates bonds and friendships that go beyond the traditional as you have experienced the birth and growth of something you all love, share and build together."

Autonomie Project, Inc.
119 Braintree Street, Suite 510
Boston, MA 02134
Phone: (877) 218-9131
Fax: (617) 440-7630
www.autonomieproject.com
www.myspace.com/autonomieproject
www.facebook.com/autonomieproject

MOUNTAINS OF THE MOON

Melissa Baswell has spent most of her life preparing to be exactly what she is right now: an award-winning designer of Mountains of the Moon Eco Fashion line, a sustainable design and apparel organization, and Melissa Baswell Eco-Luxury labels.

At age 5, Melissa was creating dolls' clothes using needle, thread and reused fabrics. In high school, she was president of the Ecology Preservation Club and wore her own handmade clothing. While a student at University of Wisconsin-Madison, she divided her free time between interning with the Environmental Education Department and sewing recycled thrift-store garments into contemporary clothing on an old hand-me-down sewing machine. "My major in college was theater," Melissa remarks. "There were a couple of required costume design classes that made me realize how much more I loved design than I did acting. I already knew how to sew, but these classes solidified everything."

Melissa has come a long way. Mountains of the Moon has the distinction of being nominated three times by Co-op America's Green Business of the Year as one of its top 10 businesses worldwide, and in October 2008, a couture dress designed by Melissa from recycled candy wrappers was exhibited at the Museum of Contemporary Art in Chicago.

Growth such as this has required enormous courage along the way.

Well before the green movement became popular, Melissa was adhering to green principles that broke the stereotyped image of "hippie" clothing as loose fitting, baggy, bland, crunchy, stiff and boring. At that time, shop owners were in doubt about the eco-friendly image. "When I started selling my ideas," she says, "all of the shop owners I visited said they really liked my designs but were hesitant about carrying them because they were eco-friendly. They were fearful that customers would stereotype and reject the clothing as not being chic fashion, and—by implication—would reject them."

It was disheartening for a young woman with a big vision, but then serendipity turned things around. She recalls,

> "Some years ago, I was particularly depressed at being rejected because eco-clothing was not accepted by the mainstream fashion industry. I was walking down a street carrying some garment bags, holding my samples, when suddenly I tripped and fell. When I stood up, there was pigeon poop all over the dress I was wearing, which, unfortunately, was part of my line that I modeled in the shops. People stopped, came over to me, staring. I was mortified because I thought they were laughing at me, but instead they started complimenting me on my dress and asked where I bought it, where they could buy it! Everything changed for me that day."

As one of very few women's designers creating classic—green—clothing today, all Melissa's inventory is green, which means it must contain all eco-friendly materials: hemp, organic, cotton, Tencel, whether new or recycled, and made in sweatshop-free factories. The garments are dyed with low-impact dyes and hang tags are printed on recycled paper, using soy ink. "Low-impact dyes have so much less impact on the environment than regular dyes," Melissa says. "They don't contain heavy metal or toxic substances; have a higher rate of absorption into the fabric (so they don't require as much chemical fixatives); require less rinsing, so there is less water waste; and require a much lower temperature for application, so energy is saved."

A few years after selling her first designs at local shops and events, she decided to create pieces that can be worn for many seasons, surpassing short-lived fads and trends that are likely to end up in landfills.

In green eco-fashion, Melissa rates herself a 9 on a scale of 1 to 10. "The only reason I don't say 10 is that I don't feel it is currently possible to be 100 percent, because somewhere down the line, products are transported by truck, plane or car, thus using fossil fuels that create a carbon footprint. However, I create the most eco-friendly products possible."

Because Melissa believes sustainable companies should give back in order to be considered truly green, her company makes regular donations, both monetary and in clothing, to several organizations, including Carbon Fund, Oxfam, Conscious Alliance, International Tibet Independence Movement, Red Door Animal Shelter, and Organic School Project. She also organizes benefits with nonprofits that raise awareness of environmental issues.

The business end of Mountains of the Moon was an additional learning curve for Melissa. She initially financed her business through credit cards, and now feels that was "an absolutely mixed blessing." On one hand, she accumulated debt that is difficult to pay off; and she was impatient, had no business experience, and didn't look into the basics of starting up. On the positive side, however, she says, "It's hard today, with the recession, to obtain any bank credit or business credit cards, so at least I do have some credit, even if it is not ideal."

Financing today is exclusively for her seasonal collection production. She has learned a great deal since the early days and shares some of her valuable insights with newcomers:

- Melissa takes pre-orders from shops and stores in the form of purchase orders
- She then presents the orders to the Chicago Apparel Industry Board (CAIB)
- CAIB checks the credit of each shop or store

- For those approved, CAIB immediately loans Melissa 60 percent of what she requested, minus a minute interest rate

- When orders are ready to ship to stores, the buyer pays CAIB directly

- The CAIB then sends Melissa the remaining 40 percent

Melissa's "Candy Dress" was chosen for display by the Museum of Contemporary Art in Chicago.

What makes Melissa a little different, at the moment, is that she does not yet have a walk-in retail shop. Her work locations are her home/office and a studio, as it is for each of her two paid part-time employees and one volunteer staff member—a work solution that cuts down their carbon footprint. Before the recession, she employed three part-timers.

Other cost-cutting measures that hold a priority for green business owners include switching from mailing hard-copy promotions and catalogs to downloadable versions from Mountains of the Moon website, or by e-mail. For customers and buyers who request hard copies, Melissa sends catalogs created from recycled materials. For shipping, she reuses her own boxes or recycled USPS boxes, which are cradle-to-cradle certified for sustainability. Waste of any kind is anathema; even leftover fabrics are used to create other projects.

Years ago she discovered her phone company, Work Assets/Credo, charged a little less than the big companies and, more important, donated to several charities, allowing their "members" to vote on which charities they would like the company to choose.

As for paid advertising, Melissa uses few of traditional media methods. She relies on the press, which contacts her and writes about her line, and this conveniently eliminates costly magazine ads.

Her website is an important low-cost marketing tool. The Internet has been a productive source of sales for Mountains of the Moon, representing about 40 percent of her sales. Internet customers can use all major credit/debit cards and pay all costs such as taxes, customs, excise, shipping or mailing. In addition, the website includes photos and descriptions of clothing, accessories and other products, including children's clothes. "We have an online mailing list of around 6,000 customers," Melissa proclaims, "and we send out monthly newsletters with special offer coupons they can use. We occasionally offer temporary sales on our website." The website also provides for downloadable catalogs and gift certificates.

The other 60 percent of sales comes from phone calls and in-person meetings, most from store/boutique owners.

She also employs public relations as a marketing tool, and hosts launch parties each season to introduce her new collections. One season included The Edie Dress, a two-tone mini made of 55 percent hemp/45 percent Tencel that could be worn by itself or over The Sophie Pants made of the same fabric. "Simple and elegant," observed one industry professional.

Special offers are another tactic she uses with great success. Melissa creates attractive recycled cardstock fliers that she and her staff pass out at events, and usually these offer a 10 percent discount.

As part of her public relations, Melissa accepts as many speaking engagements as she can. Often they are held in organic restaurants or eco-friendly bars, and she loves the opportunity to speak about her two passions: design and environmentally sound practices.

As a green designer located in Chicago, Melissa attends trade shows such as Style Max, a Chicago trade show, as a visitor, and has exhibited at the Green Festival, a retail show that takes place in Chicago and San Francisco every year. Prior to the onset of the recession, she did well and attracted new store buyers, but the effects of the economic crisis lowered her trade show sales by about 50 percent.

Melissa makes some of the higher-end items herself, because they're not made in bulk. Currently, she has a manufacturer in Denver who produces the more casual items, and one in Chicago that makes some of the higher-end pieces that she doesn't make herself. She purchases materials for her clothing lines in Colorado, California and Texas. From start to finish, Melissa's designs are patterned, dyed, manufactured and tagged in the USA, in small, 100 percent fair-labor practices facilities that are family owned and operated.

Five years from now, Melissa hopes to own a flagship shop/store that reaches deep into the mainstream. "Today," she says, "the mainstream is just becoming aware of how economics and the green movement are positively intertwined."

Mountains Of The Moon, LLC
P.O. Box 25192
Chicago, IL 60625-0192
Phone: (877) 875-0689
www.mountainsofthemoon.com

EAIRTH

Melissa Dizon was at the pinnacle of her career as design director of Levi's women's clothing for the United States, when she decided to quit not only her job, but also the frantic pace of New York. After holding challenging design positions at top-notch retailers, such as Victoria's Secret, Todd Oldham, and Levi's, Melissa relates how she "felt empty." Her burnout precipitated a life-changing decision. After some down time in Los Angeles—surfing and rediscovering her deep love of nature—she decided to return to her native Philippines to reconnect with her roots.

At the age of 7, Melissa and her siblings had made their own clothes, deconstructing their old clothes to make new designs. When she was 9, she and her family emigrated from the Philippines to New York, where she eventually studied at Otis-Parsons in Los Angeles, (formal name: Otis Art Institute of Parsons School of Design) and then Parsons in New York (formal name: Parsons The New School For Design). However, she dropped out of school after her second year after her draping teacher failed her—undeservedly, Melissa contends.

When she returned to the Philippines, she toured her country with new eyes, and discovered that her respect for the environment gave her a completely different outlook on designing clothes. "Traveling around the country, I stumbled across tribes and local crafts," Melissa explains. "I didn't mean to start a fashion brand, but my creativity went wild, patterned after the garments of Filipino tribeswomen." Melissa's aunt, who owned a successful retail shop in Manila, offered Melissa space, and suddenly Melissa was back in business with her own design house.

True to her core values and newfound fascination for her native country and its people, she branded her line Eairth, a combination of air and Earth. Serving women and men, the business would specialize in all-natural fabrics, inspired by Filipino tribal culture. Eairth clothing is a 100 percent sustainable and organic company, emphasizing the natural fibers of cotton, linen, silk, piña and abaca.

Only a few years later, Melissa has five employees and her business supports the indigenous tribes that form a small community of artisans—knitters, weavers and embroiderers. Melissa says she's "very proud of Eairth's credentials as a small, sustainable fashion retail business and the unexpected success it has had in the Philippines."

Eairth's signature comes from the innovative use of natural dyes on natural fabrics. Due to the flux characteristics of the dyes, no two pieces are identical. The following chart shows each color and its pigment source:

NATURAL COLORS	PIGMENT SOURCES
Indigo	blue indigo flowers
Khaki	wild turmeric root
Gray	fallen bark
Mauve	talisay leaves
Green	mahogany fallen wood
Rose	turmeric/indigo

NATURAL FABRICS	YARN SOURCES
Piña and tinalak	pineapple
Abaca	fiber
Cotton	banana fiber
Silk	cotton
Inabel hand-woven	silkworm

Eairth works with tribes from the north: the Ifugaos, who harvest most of the pigment sources (fallen barks, such as mahogany, tobangawan and hawili); the Tiboli from Mindanao (bark from the noni tree); and the Mangyans (talisay and duhat leaves). They extract the pigment in a process similar to "cooking in big steel vats." Most of the trees are found only in the Philippines. Pigment sources grow deep in the jungles where the tribes live. Eairth pays the tribes to gather the ingredients.

Of the natural fabrics, piña and tinalak are hand-woven on ancient looms, as is Inabel, a specialized type of weaving from the Ilocos Norte region. Cotton is the most commonly used fabric. Eairth uses it mostly for knitting jersey, and works directly with an organic cotton mill that manufactures the fabric. The company is considering a partnership with several farmers who will grow the organic cotton exclusively for Eairth. A supplier in Cebu Islands that works directly with farmers ships the piña and silk yarns to Eairth.

There are nine steps in the process:

- Tribes harvest raw pigments from jungles, seasonally

- The tribes send the pigments to Manila via boat or bus

- Eairth chops up leaves, bark, flowers

- Eairth boils and cooks each different material separately, like stew, to extract the color

- Eairth preps each garment to be individually dyed

- Eairth hand-washes each garment to remove pigment residue

- Eairth sun dries each garment

- Eairth does repairs and finishing process, which involves hand knitting, crochet and embroidery

- Eairth packs garments for shipping

The finishing process is a small cottage industry of men and women in Laguna and Bulacan. Eairth supports the community and their families—artisans for generations.

Because the by-hand process assures that two garments are identical in shape, color or even design, each one drapes to the body, creating lines that expose, wrap and/or twist naturally. Suggestive of Mangyan, Kalinga and Maranao clothing, the garment designs derive from simple geometric shapes, such as triangles, squares, and trapezoids. Details such as slashing, tearing, tucking and pulling may combine with embroideries, including lace and tatting hand-made by Belgian nuns at WUTHLE (Women United Through Handcrafted Lace and Embroidery) in Iloilo. The combinations yield a seasonal line of dresses, pants, jeans, tops, jackets and bags for women.

Melissa also designs a full line of men's sportswear—some classic, some incorporating unusual detail. Eairth's men's collections include classics and cutting-edge casual —what Melissa calls 'organic chic.' "One can wear them anywhere, depending on how you put two pieces together, to make a casual or dressy outfit," she explains.

As an example, Melissa cited a $220 T-shirt dress. To create the dress, they applied a hand-printed tribal pattern to the fabric, created draping with knots on the shoulders and added a skinny scarf with a fish design and adorned with velvet ribbons. The effect is startling and, indeed, organic chic.

Melissa's Manila showroom and studio were assembled in unique fashion. In the space she shares with her business partner and aunt, Melissa hangs pieces from her collections on hemp S-hooks attached to long racks among her aunt's antiques. It is an unusual and effective way to display the collections. The racks stand next to sewing machines used for finishing touches and alterations. Coloring and sewing teams, in addition to embroiderers, use surrounding machines to parlay their creative ideas into articles of clothing.

To stay current on industry trends, Melissa attends fashion trade shows, including Fashion Coterie and Designers and Agents in New York and Designers and Agents in Los Angeles.

Marketing consists solely of word-of-mouth efforts. Several industry critics have given her excellent reviews and featured her clothes on the Internet. Eairth has a website, and will soon add a blog. "A blog is an essential tool today," Melissa believes, "because people respond to live opinion rather than to an ad or a billboard."

Melissa's customers include socialites, bankers, artists, lawyers and entertainment and business professionals. The age group spans from 20s to mid-60s. Her high-end market, she points out, is nonetheless environmentally conscious. It is a new kind of luxury that she calls 'sustainable luxury.'

Eairth's men's collections include classics and cutting-edge casual—what Melissa terms 'organic chic'.

Eairth exported 70 percent wholesale and 30 percent retail (local Philippine sales) in 2008. By mid-2009, it was selling only 50 percent wholesale, as retail increased to the other half. With the onset of the economic crisis, the wholesale business decreased, local business flourished and Eairth switched to direct sales by booking appointments directly with stores.

In the immediate future, Melissa expects to create a range of 100 percent organic cotton dolls and a line of baby clothes inspired by a current popular doll. Other projects in the works include an online store and a distributorship, which will show the collections in Japan, and eventually her own Eairth store in Manila.

Eairth
101 Bormaheco Condominium
Metropolitan Avenue/Zapote Street
Makati City, Metro Manila, Philippines
Melissa@Eairth.org
Phone: (646) 479-4253 (U.S.)
www.eairth.ph

CHAPTER 5

SETTING UP AN ON-SITE BUSINESS

In my travels around the world, interviewing or talking with owners of all types of businesses, one observation stands out above all others: Most retailers knew they wanted to add an online store when they could afford it, while many wholesalers/distributors who sell through websites/online stores hope to open an on-site, 'brick and mortar' storefront retail shop. This is an intriguing situation.

The three parts of setting up an on-site business are the financial side, the creative side and location, location, location. Location becomes your most important decision once you have completed the financial decisions and paperwork.

But before you can begin searching for a location, you must answer many questions. Do you want to be located within a cluster of shops carrying the same type of merchandise as you? For example, a women's clothing store among many such stores—with yours as a unique green niche operation? Or would you rather be in an area that consists of numerous green shops—with yours as the sole women's clothing store? The answer will help focus your location search.

DEMOGRAPHICS

Using women's wear as an example, which female customers would your products appeal to? Only slim women? Older women? Large-size women? Juniors? Petites? What ages? What economic brackets?

To answer questions pertaining to demographics—the statistical characteristics of any given area—you need to gather as much statistical data as possible about the area's women

89

residents. What is the median income? How and where are they employed? Are they single or married? What are the average prices of their houses or rentals?

Is this a tourist area? If so, answer another set of statistical questions. What is the average number of tourists? Where do they stay? How much do they spend; and where do tourist dollars go? Is there a peak season; an off season?

The Internet turns up a wealth of demographic data, but city hall and the local chamber of commerce also provide valuable information.

TRANSPORTATION, PARKING AND FOOT TRAFFIC

Once you have gathered data on prospective sites, one way to help narrow the choices, other than the price of a lease, is to answer these questions: Is there parking behind the building if, for example, you have a furniture store or other large-item business? Is it important to have your own parking or is a nearby lot sufficient? Is there adequate street parking nearby? Is your shop's location easily accessible to cars or buses or subway/underground? How close is it to tourist buses or city bus stops? Are there pedestrian sidewalks or walkways? Is the area well lit at night? Visit the location after dark. Will the nearby parking lot remain or are there plans to convert it to condos? Is the parking lot converted into a Farmer's Market every Saturday morning? Does that create more foot traffic for you or cause noise, congestion and possibly odors?

Foot traffic is very important for many different types of businesses, but particularly for women's apparel, shoes and gift shops.

Avoid choosing a location on the basis of good to great leasing terms alone—especially in the 'wrong' end of town, or where a big-box discount store exists, or in an area with no other commercial establishments. In fact, make a list of factors in order of importance, 'must have,' 'would like' and 'not important.' Conversely, make a list of warnings that range from 'no-nos' to 'cautions.' And watch for 'right' and 'wrong' combinations. A wrong combination might be a scented candle shop that caters to the vegan lifestyle next door to a smoky wood-pit barbecued rib joint.

THE CREATIVE SIDE

Many green retail storeowners believe that because they are green, their businesses need not appeal to customers' senses or entice customers to enter and shop. "Our products are green! Shouldn't that be enough?" I have encountered this type of visual arrogance around the world. In an effort to distinguish themselves from the non-green world, the shop owner takes a wrong approach, I believe, in an attempt to appear nonconforming, different, or 'edgy'. Shop owners should not aspire to a poorly lit, careless, as-is look. No customer ever objected because a shop was too charming, too quaint or too comfortable.

A minimalist ambience—a combination of what one sees, hears, feels and smells—has no relation to the above, however. Carefully crafted, minimalism can be a desirable look.

Whether minimalist, or warm-cozy-homey, the design must be superior to a non-green competitor. Because green merchandise often costs more, due to rules and regulations governing green production, the playing field remains unlevel. Until all shoppers embrace green shopping, shopkeepers must overcome—and attempt to overtake—their non-green competitors through innovation and savvy.

Pleasing the customer's eye, no matter the type of store, is absolutely essential—even if the customer is not consciously aware of it. So, how can you create a pleasing atmosphere? Concentrate on the creative side of the business.

INTERIOR, EXTERIOR AND WINDOW DISPLAYS

Generally, the décor or look of a shop consists of three elements: equipment, display props and display materials. Equipment basics include racks, shelves and showcases. You can find a variety of styles at resale shops, recycling centers and stores going out of business or relocating.

If you intend to build shelves and racks, look for a wood house or building being torn down (call a construction or demolition company for this information). Old wood makes marvelous shelves and racks. And if you are handy, you can build a checkout or display counter to whatever shape and size you desire. An alternative to old wood is bamboo for racks and hemp for shelves; you can buy these sustainable materials at a green building supply store.

It is particularly fitting for green business owners to purchase props from secondhand stores; you can transform many items into props—and reusing and repurposing items is the green way to go.

Display props consist of items such as pieces of furniture; school, garden and household items; and old mannequins. Whether a child's desk, tables of all shapes and sizes, old luggage and trunks, apothecary cabinets or armoires, fixtures have a two-fold purpose: the primary function is to display merchandise and the secondary purpose is to resell when you no longer need them.

Regardless of the type of retail business you have, you can almost always use—and subsequently resell—props.

Display materials, on the other hand, need not cost anything—a bowl of lemons from your lemon tree, a pile of different kinds of squash from your garden, nuts or berries that fall from trees, autumn leaves, a few branches of pussy willows in a tall decorated can, old books, toys, hardware and kitchen items and things from your own home all offer interesting options for window displays that catch the eye and showcase your merchandise. Windows should captivate lookie-loos and lure them inside.

Vignettes—small arrangements of merchandise—create a distinctive setting, emphasizing how your merchandise works together, or coordinates, hopefully enticing customers to buy multiple pieces.

THE FINANCIAL SIDE

Financially speaking, first and most important, you must have funding for at least two years—the common length of time it takes to start up. To gain a foundation of basic business practices, if you have never been a business owner, look to SCORE for its vast number of volunteers, one-on-one professional counselors from your field who conduct symposiums and workshops.

You can also learn the management basics from private companies that advertise on the Internet, adult evening classes and daytime college courses. But SCORE offers more information and help.

Besides the overall business plan discussed in "Setting Up an Internet Business" (chapter 4), a merchandise purchasing plan—buying to your forecast—is also essential.

An open-to-buy, or OTB, is a budget specifically designed to manage the purchase of new merchandise. It is calculated for each buying season in each category of goods. There are countless articles, blogs, videos, books and software applications to guide business owners in OTB budgeting. The method you select is up to you. You may use a generic method, or find one customized for your industry, but regardless of the method it is an essential tool for retail shop owners. Without it inventory control can quickly go out of control.

FINANCING

As you will read in forthcoming chapters, the majority of owners start up small, thereby using only savings and credit cards. But as your business becomes successful, or has large start-up costs, you may need a loan—if not from family or friends, a bank. A neighborhood bank (as close as possible to your business), a credit union or Small Business Administration (SBA) are your best choices. Part of their philosophy is to lend to businesses in their neighborhood first—a kind of "good neighbor policy."

The following are other important topics that will be discussed at SCORE workshops:

- Legal Matters

- Accounting and Bookkeeping

- Licenses

- Trademarks

- Zoning

- Insurance

∽

After studying many green retail businesses, I am convinced that a corresponding online business is essential—even mandatory—to reach every customer possible, thereby making every possible dollar. Furthermore, your online presence makes it easier for customers to find your on-site business.

For in-depth information on these subjects and more see *The Specialty Shop: How to Create Your Own Unique and Profitable Retail Business*, by Dorothy Finell, AMACOM Books ©2007

GREEN GENES

Green Genes, a baby and young children's shop in Chicago's Andersonville neighborhood, heralded its opening on Earth Day, March 28, 2008. It was founded by best friends and partners, Heather Muenstermann and Christina Isperdul, who are passionate about the environment and teaching a green way of life to their customers who, in turn, pass it on to their children.

Heather is a former nanny and children's art therapist. Her career credentials also include managing a Baby Gap shop and working in mental health and as personal shopper at F.A.O. Schwartz, the latter two in Chicago. Summers, during college, she worked at Disneyland. Many people who know the always-smiling Heather know her shop, business sense, integrity, patience, joyful friendliness, and desire to impart information—all the qualities of a perfect proprietor.

Andersonville is a close-knit community that supports its small businesses and many of the young families in the area possess an eco-conscious philosophy. An organization called eco-Andersonville promotes and encourages an environmental, economic and social sustainability. To that end, they developed the eco-Andersonville Certified Business Award which includes the following criteria: Creation of a green work place that reduces usage of energy, water, hazardous and toxic materials, and maximizes recycling and waste reduction. Green Genes fits that prototype extremely well.

When Heather and Christina leased the 1,100-square-foot premises, they chose low-VOC (Volatile Organic Compounds) paints, laid bamboo floors and used Kirei board—a sustainable material from the leftover stalks of sorghum plants—for the

95

counter where all business transactions occur. Antiques and second-hand pieces were bought for store fixtures and displays (frequently sold to customers). Bureaus and assorted furniture of different sizes and shapes are all utilized as displays for merchandise: cabinets with open apothecary tops, hutch tops, end tables, bookcases, commodes with child-size pull-out wash basins, suitcases and steamer trunks, wood potty chairs, and children's tables and chairs. The few build-outs were created by refinishing discarded lumber and scraps. They use CFL (compact fluorescent lamp) bulbs in small decorative light fixtures throughout the store and plan to change to track lighting with more eco-friendly illumination.

Bureaus, cabinets, hutch tops, end tables, and bookcases are utilized for displaying merchandise, creating a cozy interior and a second life for furniture.

The interior atmosphere is bright and lively, and customers entering the shop immediately experience its homey ambiance. Even the restroom, with the changing table for babies and walls covered with children's paintings and photos, is charming and cozy.

Their standout window displays create a three-dimensional illusion, drawing onlookers. Layers of merchandise interspersed with rectangular tins of grasses (changed with the seasons) create an aura of warmth, hominess, and coziness—implying home, family, love and happiness. A window displayer designs the windows but Heather executes the designs.

The storeroom, beyond the selling area, features recycled shelves to store extra merchandise in multi-sized plastic bins—neatly numbered, easily accessible, and stacked in orderly fashion from floor to within arm's reach. The storeroom is large enough to be easily converted into an extension of selling space, as needed.

For start-up funds the two partners merged some of their own savings but the majority of financing came from a Small Business Administration loan through a local bank that was particularly interested in helping women-owned local businesses.

Green Genes carries a wide variety of green products for babies, children and adults, in many categories and by many makers. In keeping with the green philosophy, it also carries second-hand items. The variety includes:

- Clothing and blankets—made from organic cotton, soy fibers, bamboo, and hemp; from Chapter One Organics, Wondertoast, A Little Lark, Pluto, Baby Soy, Speesees, Kice Kice, Positively Organic, New Jammies, Kicky Pants, Kiddopotamus and Sprout

- Toys, games and blocks—U.S.-made wood toys; Fair Trade; hand-knit toys; tea sets; dishes and trucks made from recycled milk jugs, rocket ships and teepees made from recycled cardboard by ImagiPLAY; Barefoot Books; Maple Landmark; Educo, a brand of HaPe Toys; and Camden Rose

- Art and art supplies—local artists' works; art printed on organic linen, hemp and cotton canvases; organic and natural art supplies and recycled paper sketchbooks; mobiles by Petite Collage

- Diaper bags and totes—backpack and tote styles; PVC-free and/or made from recycled materials by Kalencom, Fleurville and Envirosax

- Bath and body products—for children and adults: organic (some certified U.S. organic) and paraben-free by Goodies by Erbaviva, Noodle & Boo, Deep Steep and Clean Well

- Candles—soy with organic cotton wicks and recycled glass containers

- Cards and notebooks—made of recycled paper. Smock cards use bamboo paper and 100 percent wind energy production.

- Baby bottles, water bottles, teethers and pacifiers— BPA-free, PVC-free, phthalate-free plastic bottles* as well as biodegradable glass bottles, surround by an easy-to-hold silicon sleeve by WeeGo, Green to Grow, Natursutten and Sofie the Giraffe. (*Regular plastic bottles discharge three known toxic chemicals when exposed to heat.)

The company also carries diapers, specifically gDiapers, made in Australia, which consist of a reusable cotton cover and a plastic-free, biodegradable snap-in liner that can be flushed or composted.

 ∽

When the partners stumble upon fantastic finds, the second-hand items are cleaned and repaired as necessary. They collect damaged or defective (but still useful) items and donate them to local organizations, such as a women and children's shelter. "Our thought was, 'Why let gently used items be discarded when they still have plenty of life in them?'" Heather questions. She recalls this story:

> "Taking advantage of a quiet moment in the shop, I immersed myself in e-mail catch-up. Apparently so engrossed in correspondence, I didn't realize that I had accidentally pushed the panic button, something to be used only in dire

emergencies. Suddenly, there were two plainclothes officers rushing into my store. 'Are you okay? Are you sure you're okay?' they asked, trying to read my eyes, no doubt assuming someone was hiding behind the counter with me, potentially with a weapon. Once we all realized what had happened and had a good laugh, the officers glanced around the store. 'Hey, this is a really cute place. Mind if we look around?' The gentlemen were browsing through the store when I heard them ooh-ing and aah-ing. They were admiring a fantastic 'second-hand-but-looks-brand-new' fire truck that we had recently added to our inventory. After some discussion, one of the officers felt his grandchild would be the perfect recipient of the fire truck, and he said he would get back to me. They left, and shortly thereafter, he called to say he'd be back in a few days to purchase it, which he did—but not without a lot of teasing to suggest I had intentionally pushed the panic button to lure potential shoppers into the store!"

In line with their 100 percent green policy, Heather assures, "We purchase products from several places. We start locally, in Chicago, and then expand to the rest of the country." Products from outside the United States must meet Green Genes criteria: organic, sustainably-produced, fair trade, and upcycled—a component of sustainability using waste materials in new products that reduces waste and virgin material.

Heather is service-oriented to an unusually high degree. A customer once came into the store with a baby swing—purchased elsewhere—and told Heather she was worried that she was not using the swing properly. Heather promptly explained the problem and found a video to show her.

No matter how inexpensive a gift, Green Genes makes it extra special by using wonderful gift-wrapping materials: two tissues, blue and green, in a box with a Green Genes label, tied with cotton ribbon, a gift tag attached by a hemp string, and placed in a bag with Green Genes' name printed in low-dye colors. All gift-wrappings are recycled and/or biodegradable.

Using wrapping paper with a shop logo on it is an excellent marketing strategy for businesses.

Christina, a software engineer, has connections at a local company that produces software for "point of sale" systems. Serendipitously, the store acquired the software for their cash register system. Christina handles the operational aspect s of the business, paying most bills electronically, to cut down on paper. Additional energy-saving methods include using printer paper on both sides where possible, and using recycled material for shipping. The business recycles cardboard, batteries, light bulbs, plastics and items that customers bring into the store, such as plastic water bottles and take-out containers.

Green Genes' beautiful gift-wrap is an important marketing tool.

Their best means for attracting potential customers is social networking sites, such as Facebook and Twitter, and people who read their reviews on Yelp.com. When they receive solicitations for fundraisers and events, they make their decision based on specific target audiences and then donate to those causes. And, of course, they take full advantage of the free press that they receive. "We have been fortunate to have many people write about Green Genes on their blogs and websites, which drives a good deal of traffic our way," Heather observes. Conversely, the partners have been asked to sit on several speaking panels at eco-friendly events and seminars.

Periodically, they schedule special events, often timed for the holidays. They host a wonderful mix of readings by local book authors, arts and crafts mornings or afternoons for children, composting demonstrations, organic baby food tastings and special late-night events with wine and cheese. A community outreach event becomes an opportunity to bring customers into the store increasing business prominence.

Heather's advice to retailers-to-be or those in the first stages of a startup: Follow the same first steps she and her partner used, and in much the same step-by-step manner. "Most important," she advises, "is a well-thought-out business plan. We found that to be essentially a blueprint for moving forward. Next, we visited the SBA website and used a suggested business plan—a downloadable template—to help us get started." To achieve this, the SBA recommended the partners seek counsel from SCORE, an association of business professionals, usually retired, who volunteer to meet with people, offer business advice and even offer follow-up sessions. (To take the SCORE course in person, check online for the nearest SCORE office, or check with an SBA-authorized bank.) "Next we met with our local chamber of commerce to discuss local demographics, and the needs and desires of the neighborhood," Heather continues.

The demographics are an important factor in any marketing program and affect almost all aspects of a business. A 2008 market study in Andersonville—including households within a five-minute drive of Andersonville—showed a population of 105,305. The demographics for age, economics, and marital status were complementary to Green Genes' goals. More importantly, Heather, who has lived in the area for 10 years, knew from her own research that the area was eco-conscious, an essential factor for any prospective green retailer when choosing a location.

For any business owner, green or otherwise, "It is absolutely vital to have a passion for the business you intend to create, but there must be a demand for it as well." Heather adds, "Along the way, it was easy to become overwhelmed and confused, but that's when we had to just step back briefly and take things one step at a time."

Regarding the future of their business, Heather says they'd like to have a strong online presence for e-commerce and a second retail operation. But long before that, they hope to do lots of business, which would mean adding additional staff.

Green Genes
5111 N. Clark St.
Chicago, IL 60640
Phone: (773) 944-9250
www.green-genes.com

CHAPTER 6

CONSTRUCTION

The general subject of green construction encompasses many aspects of the trade: products, materials and ancillary products and services such as architecture, paints and lighting. Fans and appliances are also part of the overall construction picture.

Entrepreneurs considering launching a green business, or adopting green concepts in an established business, should become familiar with the possibilities for green interior and exterior construction. Those who are already in construction or its many related industries—from architects to painters, roofers to landscapers—will find that consumers increasingly want green ideas and materials.

Hundreds of new green construction products appear on the market every year, especially since 2000. Now, they are proliferating. One seems to read or hear about emerging products every week. They debut worldwide, and there are too many to mention here.

∽

Stronger and lighter than wood, hemp is manufactured for a variety of products. For example, fiberboard could replace timber, reducing the need to destroy forests.

Hemp consists of a stem whose outer part, or skin, contains long fibers and two hollow wood-like cores. Stems are processed into two materials, hurds and fibers. Both have properties that are used in building construction. (*Building With Hemp* by Steve Allin)

The strength, flexibility and economy of hemp for the construction of residential and commercial buildings offer several practical applications. Products including fiberboard, wallboard and paneling, as well as roof tiles and insulation, can be produced with hurds so absorbent that they can hold five times their weight in water. Lime, sand, plaster and stone cement are added to hemp hurds with enough water to dampen the materials. The resulting mixture, "hempcrete," is poured into hemp plywood frames. (Similar combinations are marketed as Canobiote, Canosmose and Isochanvre.)

Hempcrete, according to some reports, can be seven times stronger and three times more pliable than similar building materials; it is, therefore, considered an ideal material for earthquake zones: fireproof, waterproof, weather-resistant and self-insulating. Pipes can also be made from hempcrete, adding a crack-resistant quality.

Heating and compressing plant fibers creates inexpensive fire-resistant materials with thermal and sound-insulating qualities. These fiber materials could replace drywall and wood paneling.

Another building material, plaster, acts as insulation when combined with hemp, which is mixed with lime and cast in wooden frames or sprayed against wood or stone. And there are also no-VOC, hemp-based paints that are said to offer effective coating and durability.

࿓

Autoclaved Aerated Concrete, a building material created in Sweden in 1912 and since used in Europe, has surfaced in Monterey County, California. A combination of cement, lime, sand, fly ash, water and aluminum powder, the mixture, expands up to five times its original volume. Then it is poured into molds to create blocks held together with rebar. They create walls, panels and roofs, over which plaster or a stucco compound is applied. (Sarah Kenoyer, "Concrete Progress," Monterey County Weekly)

Several houses in Pebble Beach and Carmel, California were constructed with the product, thanks to custom home designer Dave Wilday, who heard about the material in 1970. It is lightweight, has super strength and resists mold and termites. It has insulating qualities that considerably reduce heating and cooling energy use and completely avoids traditional toxic insulation. It is also fire-resistant and, according to a Pebble Beach homeowner, soundproof.

∽

One of the strongest materials in the world, bamboo has come a long way as a construction material. No longer used only for scaffolding and structural supports in Asia and other countries, it is now in a period of renaissance that may well affect the United States and Europe. In 2001, at the International Bamboo Housing Workshop in Mizoram, India, ideas emerged to develop new futuristic materials as technology makes more options possible.

India took the lead in developing bamboo products, which is interesting because China and other Asian countries were leaders for centuries. Indian Plywood Industries Training Institute in Bangalore already markets bamboo mat roofing products.

As timber becomes less plentiful, bamboo could become a construction alternative because so many products have been, or are in the process of being, developed and marketed.

Among bamboo building products are mat boards, manufactured by converting bamboo slices into slivers, then weaving and finally hot-pressing. Mat boards are far superior to plywood. Plyboards are composed of a mixture of bamboo mats and slivers, hot-pressed; the benefit is the boards can be waterproofed.

Even caulking can be produced by using shredded bamboo from culms, embedded in a putty of lime and tung oil.

Bamboo boards are processed by machine. The manufacturing process involves gluing and hot-pressing flattened strips. The boards can be used for almost all purposes in place of wood, and could prove superior due to their strength and longevity.

The Bamboo Development Agency in Mizoram (a center for bamboo manufacturing and products) has been developing bamboo concrete technology as a future product.

An example of bamboo's strength and durability is in buildings in Costa Rica that withstood two huge earthquakes, while buildings made of other materials collapsed.

Exterior uses include reinforcement for concrete and adobe, roofing, framing and scaffolding, awnings, irrigation pipes, drainage and bilge pumps, wood-type shingles and walls. In addition, bamboo has a role in landscaping, gardening, tennis courts, pools and greenhouses.

Interior uses include walls, tile flooring, matting, storage and bookcases, light-bulb filaments, caulking, various types of hinges and joints and a plethora of furnishings and textiles.

❧

Other materials in a commercial building or house include glass and stainless steel. The products found in a kitchen, such as new or recycled cabinets, for example, contain materials like formaldehyde-free FSC-certified woods, such as cherry, maple, oak and alder, as well as bamboo and wheatboard, the relatively new material made of recycled wheat stalk and straw. Countertop options include IceStone (a combination of recycled glass chips in concrete), Eurostone (quartz chips in a resin binder) and ShetkaStone (recycled paper in a formaldehyde-free resin base). Granite and marble are two popular choices for countertops because they are natural and durable. But these stones, quarried from the earth, are unsustainable because once harvested no re-growth can occur.

❧

Cork is an excellent kitchen flooring material—practical and easy to clean. It resists mold and absorbs sound, and is hypoallergenic and soft under foot.

Cork is the outer bark of the Cork Oak tree, harvested directly from the tree and allowing new bark to grow in its place. Every tree is a renewable source of the raw material—an excellent example of a natural, sustainable product.

The first harvest of cork bark is about 20 years after saplings are planted; therefore, a harvest occurs approximately every 10 years. For the next 200 years or so, cork bark will be peeled from each tree each time. At the end of that period, two saplings can be planted within the same space ensuring a cork forest expands with time. In addition, a Cork Oak reproduces naturally via falling acorns that seed themselves and mature, thus reinforcing expansion.

The world's major Cork Oak forests are in Portugal, Spain, France and North African countries, with Portugal accounting for about 50 percent. A combination of the microclimate (precise rainfall and wind conditions) and soil type that exist in the Mediterranean region offer perfect conditions for growth.

Wine bottle corks are not the only products of cork. In addition are the following: floor and wall tiles, wallpaper, furniture, fabrics, shoe soles and insoles, buoys and floats, fishing rod handles, gaskets, joint fillers, bottle stoppers and bulletin boards.

Lightweight, flexible, durable, rot-resistant, dust-absorbent, and fire-resistant in its natural state, cork has one of the best insulating and acoustical properties of all substances.

∽

Stainless steel is considered green because it is 100 percent recyclable, melted innumerable times into many new rustless products. In fact, more than 5 percent of new stainless comes from recycled stainless. Its alloy composition—the base metal naturally resists corrosion—accounts for its long life span. For this reason, stainless steel cookware, sinks and countertops enhance hygiene in restaurants and public kitchens.

∽

Jars, bottles and other glass containers can be broken into small pieces, or cullet, which melts at a lower temperature, so as more is added to a mixture of raw materials, it needs less energy to melt. As a comparison, throwaway bottles consume three times as much energy as reusables; 12 to 15 percent of glass used in the United States alone is recycled and the figure increases every year.

When glass is produced from only raw materials, the energy consumed is three times higher and related water pollution 50 percent higher. The number of throwaway glass containers was about 28 billion before September 11, 2001, according to Earthworks Group. That is enough to fill both World Trade Center Towers every two weeks. (www.sustainabilitymatters.net.au)

Not recyclable are, for instance, windowpanes, light bulbs and cookware, because they combine ceramics and glass, which would introduce impurities into the recycling process.

The relatively new Glass AGG System, used by Glass Aggregate Systems of Australia, converts waste glass, including plate and laminated window glass, into "glass aggregate fines" in various sizes for various uses. The fines are used for road base aggregate, concrete additives, septic tank drains, sand blasting, hydroponics, landscaping and other purposes.

❧

Clearly, green construction is in extensive use around the world—from villages in underdeveloped countries to the finest buildings in cosmopolitan cities. In the United States, scores of major organizations oversee the growth and quality of green construction; dozens of magazines and newsletters devote their content to development information; and thousands of smaller entities across the country, such as chambers of commerce, promote sustainable construction materials to local business owners.

❧

'Green architects' (that is what the dedicated ones call themselves) feature prominently in this book because they are the visionaries who make green buildings and houses a reality.

They are also the people who research and seek green products—architecturally safe and suitable—for building or rebuilding structures. Equally important, they build with an eye toward the building's waste materials when the time arrives to demolish (or restore) it years down the road.

They order a multitude of products—from individual components to integrated systems—from green manufacturers, wholesalers and distributors. Green architects are instrumental in creating the demand for green products.

While manufacturers create the green products from raw materials, green architects envision the designs and green contractors execute to the specifications—and submit orders for those products.

For these reasons, green architects and builders play an integral role in this book.

CARMEL DEVELOPMENT COMPANY

Michael Waxer is a California-based architect—a green architect who devotes his work and life to sustainability. A Massachusetts Institute of Technology graduate and vice president of Carmel Development Company, Michael asserts that the ideal building material for a house or commercial structure is found, harvested and used on the site and ultimately returned to the site at the end of the structure's usefulness.

"If a home is built where naturally occurring stone exists, using that stone within the home as a structural material, a finish material, or crushed as an aggregate in concrete, the home is a sustainable structure," explains Michael, who devotes his being to sustainability. "A material that requires little or no maintenance and lasts the lifetime of the building, such as glass, is preferable."

The developer of exclusive luxury communities holds Green Leadership Certification, served on the board of The Sustainability Academy since 2006 and presides over the American Institute of Architects (AIA) Monterey Bay Chapter. His own green home and office are located near the gates of Tehama, Clint Eastwood's golf club community, which Michael's firm helped develop.

With his depth of experience, Michael, when planning the construction of a green property, asks important questions, such as:

- Is the material abundant and naturally occurring (e.g. cork)?

- Is the material made from a waste product (e.g. rubber flooring made from recycled tires or carpet made from recycled plastic)?

- Does the material meet a recognized standard that, in the case of wood, assures it is sustainably harvested (e.g. FSC Certification for wood products)?

- Is the material produced and/or fabricated in the immediate region where the building is being proposed?

- He notes two other criteria regarding nonflammable materials:

- By using nonflammable roofing materials, a Class A roof will provide more time to flee a house or fight a fire.

- Use nonflammable exterior wall materials, such as stone, which provides superior protection. And, because heat travels up a wall, selecting overhang and soffit materials becomes especially important.

Also among Michael's primary considerations when designing a house or commercial building is lighting, or daylighting. In the Northern Hemisphere, north-facing windows (or glass) provide light without glare because the sun's path only indirectly shines through north-facing glazing. This holds true for skylights and tubular daylighting devices installed on a north-facing roof. The use of high-opening windows on the north side can provide the dual goals of providing daylight and an escape for excess warm and hot air.

Daylight for a kitchen has different criteria. Positioning work surfaces and sinks underneath windows will enable natural light to help minimize the use of heat during cold months. Maximize the number of windows facing south for the sun's energy during winter in the Northern Hemisphere.

For additional lighting, and at night, use of LED (light-emitting diodes) lighting represents the newest generation of lumens (the measurement of light that refers to efficiency). A rheostat for dimming can easily control this flexible lighting. With LED bulbs, fixtures have a longer lifetime better than with fluorescent lighting—without the toxic mercury. Early LED lights focused on maximizing efficiency, which resulted in the quality of light being white and stark. Second-generation LED bulbs, however, incorporate warmer colors, approximating natural sunshine's yellow glow.

Carmel stone arches of Clint Eastwood's Tehama clubhouse.

If materials are the first consideration in designing a new structure, and the second is lighting, then the third is water: It is possible that water-conserving fixtures and appliances, considered deluxe today, will soon become standard. These include high-efficiency toilets, with or without dual flush; low-flow showerheads with integrated shut-off valves; and aerators for sinks—all of which reduce flow. Many new washing machines were designed for minimal water usage.

However, outdoor water use often exceeds total indoor usage, Michael warns. He suggests landscaping with native and drought-tolerant plantings—not only to conserve water, but also to minimize risk of fire. Rainwater catchment systems are important to store runoff from autumn and winter for use during drier months.

Michael's hypothetical dream home would start with a concrete foundation, sustainable if it has a certain amount of Fly Ash, a waste product of coal power plants that can reduce the amount of cement in concrete by 20 percent. Another ingredient of concrete is steel containing at least 30 percent recycled steel, which Michael recommends in certain situations; it is appropriate because it uses all-natural elements and is fireproof.

For the frame, he would choose FSC lumber to ensure a sustainable product; he would use the same material for beams, girders and roof rafters. For insulating wood walls, he would use spray-in foam—excellent also for filling cracks, with the additional benefits of controlling noise, moisture and mold. Michael would also accept Blue Jeans (recycled jeans) insulation or insulated concrete forms. ICFs, he says, are easy to assemble on site; concrete is poured into forms. The insulation is already part of the forming system, so it requires no additional insulation. He would choose clay tiles on the sloped section of the roof. On the flat section, he would install four solar thermal panels and 500 square feet of solar electric.

He lists all other materials or products in three categories (below) to achieve StepUp2Green, or SU2G, certification for middle-class homeowners. Unlike LEED—the most rigid, complex, costly, and prestigious of the certification programs, mostly allied with businesses, BuildItGreen's system and the National Association of Home Builders' green building standards, SU2G targets middle-class homeowners who want to go green on low budgets.

Within these categories, look for Energy Star, a system created with U.S. taxpayer money to set efficiency standards for many electric conveniences in homes and businesses. The memorable Energy Star logo, affixed to items that meet the standards, helps consumers select the efficient electrical items. This reduces energy bills and fosters a green marketplace. Although stringent product testing increases the cost of these products, manufacturers understand the value of gaining consumer recognition of green products.

Here are the three categories:

ENERGY SAVING DEVICES

- Motion detectors and LED bulbs on outdoor fixtures, entryways and bathrooms

- Furnace, AFUE, natural gas or propane, Energy Star labeled

- Windows and glass doors, double-pane, central air conditioning only if needed or one single-room Energy Star-labeled unit with built-in timer

- Hot water, two-panel solar thermal system

- Renewable energy with a photovoltaic (PV) or wind energy system

- Heat and power fuel cell combination such as renewable energy geothermal heat pump

WATER SAVINGS DEVICES

- Water heater, Energy Star, whole house tankless gas (on-demand) and recirculating hot water system with timer and remote start

- Irrigation, sprinklers for turf areas with Evapo-Transpiration (ET) smart controller

OVERALL IMPROVEMENTS

- Ceiling fans (if no air conditioning installed), Energy Star, in as many rooms as possible

- Window coverings, interior and exterior, more than one-quarter-inch thick for all windows and skylights (operable so they can close at night)

- ❧ Fireplaces with glass doors completely covering opening (or fixed glass front gas fireplace appliances)

- ❧ Appliances, all Energy Star labeled

- ❧ Decking, FSC-certified wood or natural stone

Although not included as construction products, Michael recommends the use of LCD and Energy Star certified television and computer screens; self-charging smoke alarms that can screw into light fixtures (no batteries necessary); kitchens equipped with fire extinguisher and carbon monoxide alarms, along with smoke alarms in bedrooms, hallways and on each level, including the basement.

The last step in the completion of a building project is usually exterior and interior painting. Green paint products eliminate volatile organic compounds from the products.

Home and business owners thrive buying from green businesses a little at a time—products like no-VOC paints and Energy Star appliances. The more buyers, the more green businesses, the more people employed, and the more new green products appearing in the marketplace.

"A home can be designed not just as net-zero energy, but can actually be energy positive and regenerative," Michael assures. "Regenerative architecture is designed to be sustainable for all time."

Carmel Development Company
Post Office Box 450
Carmel, CA 93921
Phone:(831) 625-1066
Fax:(831) 625-6220
mlwaxer@carmeldevelopment.com

ENVIRO INTERNATIONAL

A construction project usually starts with an architect who chooses the products he or she wants used. An architect dedicated to green concepts will use green materials and products if they are available and of an acceptable, or preferably superior quality, which they usually are.

Two houses and a church encapsulate the green building philosophy of Carmel, California-based architect and builder Safwat Malek, founder of Enviro International and member of the U.S. Green Building Council and Carmel Green Building Committee. Enviro International's green building techniques and innovative design offer distinctive function and style for commercial buildings, resorts and residential developments.

Safwat is something of a pioneer in the movement, asserting the idea of sustainable architecture in his 1966 master's thesis, Industrialization of the Building Industry, at Edinburgh University, Scotland. He began encouraging, then promoting, and ultimately applying resource conservation to the building industry. He uses only green products, such as sustainable lumber; nontoxic paints; and energy-efficient appliances, heating and electrical materials.

In 2001, Safwat designed and built his first totally green house in Los Altos Hills, California, using these materials—all produced with recycling in mind:

- FSC lumber for framing of walls and floors; framing created a seismic-compliant structure

- Straw bales used as infill for the exterior (which Safwat would not use again because they were expensive and impractical for the size and type of house)

- Seamed metal roof

- Photovoltaic panels

- Solar energy storage batteries

- Pellet stoves for supplemental space heating

- Recycled lumber from "deconstruction" of house

- Green roof—Living Roof—installed on flat portion of roof

In a 2007 remodel, where the house was deconstructed, Safwat used:

- Salvaged lumber from the gutted house to reuse in the reconstruction

- Solar panels of translucent glass (blocking UV rays)

- Salvaged concrete—crushed pieces, held in place with dry sand, to extend the driveway

Safwat choose energy and water-efficient systems for interior and exterior:

INTERIOR

- Dual-flush toilets.

- Hot water heater, 92 percent efficient

- Radiant-heated floors constructed over concrete slabs (with heat contained in water tubes)

- Energy Star high-efficiency furnace for space heating

- Travertine tile

- Low-voltage lighting with dimmers throughout

EXTERIOR

- Indigenous plants with drip system

- Rainwater collection system

The rainwater collection system is a network of pipes connected underground culminating in a cistern. The water collected is used for irrigation of plants, grass, and the roof garden of deciduous plants and planter boxes

"My reason for buying that particular property," recalls Safwat, "was because it was already a duplex, meaning that the buyer would have a choice of a one- or two-family home that easily could convert at any time."

The house earned Build It Green and Energy Star certifications.

Custom-designed solar panels by Safwat Malek also serve as an interior skylight. Roof garden takes advantage of sunlight and views.

The Unitarian Universalist Church in Carmel presented a different type of challenge. It sought to triple its size, and was adamant that the expansion be green. "Because the master plan called for a new sanctuary accommodating 550 seats, a library, classrooms, new administration offices and lobby, based on the cost of the project and available funds, we decided to divide the project into different phases," Safwat recalls.

Construction started on Phase 1, which included all site work (grading, storm system, exterior lighting grid with parking lights, fire lines, fire hydrants, site retaining walls, foundations, structural retaining walls, and under-slab plumbing). Between 2007 and 2008, they installed a photovoltaic (PV) solar system, the largest of its kind on the Monterey Peninsula at that time.

Prior to starting the addition, Safwat registered with the USGBC (United States Green Building Council) monitoring and documenting all activities of Phase 1. Once he completes the project, the church will apply for LEED Silver Certification.

"In order to claim a building 'green,' it must be verified by a credible third-party organization," Safwat explains. "Otherwise, one could claim to be or to have done anything and nobody could dispute it, which is considered 'greenwashing,' A third party that has the accreditation must be able to say, 'I can prove it to you with these photos and documents showing the what, why, when and where and how.'"

Here is a sample of the materials Safwat needed to document for the church's application for LEED Certification:

- Fly ash in concrete
- All recyclable materials were taken to and weighed at recycling facilities (naming the materials)
- All construction materials were documented for recycling content (listing materials)
- All storm drain pipes were collected and deposited in underground drain collection system (noting the number of pipes)
- Bike racks and signs were made of recycled materials

Sources of some products Safwat mentioned are:

THERMAL REFLECTIVE PAINTS (CERAMIC POWDER ADDITIVE)

- Insuladd
- Hy-Tech

    ❧ Rhino Shield California

SOUNDPROOF THERMAL REFLECTIVE GLASS

    ❧ Spectrum Industries

    ❧ Alibaba

SOLAR HOT WATER SYSTEM/SOLAR POOL HEATING

    ❧ Radiantec

    ❧ Sun Grabber

    ❧ Solar Hot USA

    ❧ Solar Roofs

The recession that began in 2007 affected the church's funding, and Safwat's firm stopped working after it completed Phase 1. The church plans another capital campaign and will begin Phase 2 soon.

Enviro International
Post Office Box 1734
Pebble Beach, CA 93953
Phone: (831) 626-3490
Fax: (831) 626-5401
SafwatMalek@enviro-international.com
www.enviro-international.com

MCA TILE

Maruhachi Ceramics of America, MCA Tile, has updated the ancient natural clay tiles used 5,000 years ago in China, the Middle East, Greece and Rome to clay tiles called 'cool clay tiles' or 'cool roof.' Clay roofing surfaced in America with the first English immigrants then moved across the country to California and Texas for the roofs of Missions built by Spanish priests.

Yoshihiro Suzuki, or Yoshi as he is called, president and CEO of MCA received the first Energy Star Certification for clay roofing tile in the United States in December, 2002, and is LEED certified. Yoshi was born in Japan and came to the United States in 1972. He graduated from California State University, Sacramento, in 1977. He opened a feasibility study office for a clay roof tile factory in Norwalk, California in 1983, after which he started MCA. In 1985, using personal funds, he opened another clay tile factory in Corona, California, where he and 45 employees are still located.

"When I started the business there were nine specialized tile companies in the United States and now there are only five," Yoshi says.

MCA developed modern, eco-friendly manufacturing techniques to manipulate the thermal clay, which contains complex, inorganic color pigments that gain solar reflectance. To add color to the clay tile surface, a matte glazed process is applied before it is kiln fired because pigments, atmosphere and firing temperature all affect the final color. 'Cool roof' (Cool Rating Council) colors range from dark brown to white, and increase the effectiveness of cooling or heating.

One of a group of tests Dr. William Miller conducted on cool roof tiles showed that they had low heat flux resulting in cooler attic temperatures in summer and warmer temperatures in winter. Dr. Miller's research was included in a 2006 report prepared for the Oak Ridge National Laboratory (ORNL) for the United States Department of Energy. Other tests showed that after three years of exposure the clay roof tiles met or exceeded California's Title 24 cool roof standard of 40 percent solar reflectance and thermal emittance requirements.

The waste product from tile manufacturing, a crushed roof tile powder, called 'grog', is mixed with soil and donated by Yoshi to baseball fields or tennis courts in his local area. It is his way of "giving back" to his local community.

Custom House, Kaneohe Bay, Hawaii shows off a handsome roof of Weathered Green Blend tile.

Sales from oversees buyers present no problems because he requires a letter of credit (L/C) from the buyer's bank or 100 percent prepayment.

In addition to the MCA website, Yoshi advertises in trade magazines and distributes a printed catalogue to customers and potential customers at the two trade shows he attends each year: Pacific Coast Building Conference (PCBC) in San Francisco and Western States Roofing Trade Show.

MCA hosts an open house and presents special offers occasionally as well as conducting factory tours (by appointment only) and distributing local flyers for public relations purposes.

MCA's tiles/roofs adorn elegant buildings, such as the Bellagio Hotel in Las Vegas, the First Hawaiian Bank in Honolulu, Kapolei Entertainment Center and the Memorial Hermann Institute in Houston, Texas.

Beyond the United States, MCA has shipped custom tiles, with the exact specified color, to Japan, Kuwait and Saudi Arabia—the last two countries "after the Persian Gulf War," Yoshi notes, "because so many commercial and high-end homes were damaged."

MCA Tile
1985 Sampson Ave.
Corona, CA 92879
Phone: (800) 736-6221
Phone: (951) 736-9590
Fax: (951) 736-6052
www.mca-tile.com

MUDCRAFTERS

Even as a child, Talmath Lakai, of MudCrafters Construction, had a passion for playing in dirt and mud, and helping his stepfather on construction jobs. Years later, he studied the art of adobe floors and mud plaster walls.

As a first step in creating adobe flooring, Talmath mixed 75 percent sharp sand and 25 percent finely screened clay with enough water in a wheelbarrow to achieve a pancake-batter consistency. In the next step, he threw in several handfuls of chopped straw and poured the "batter" over a tamped road base (a mixture of gravel and sand) to bind the materials. The third step was leveling the pour for smoothness, followed by pressing the mix with the trowel to harden it for durability and allow the clay content to surface.

At this point, Talmath poured what was now wet adobe over in-floor radiant heat tubes. Next, he added a coating of thin layers of natural-colored clay, after which he started polishing or burnishing the floor with a mix of several natural colors. "I was always on the lookout for clays of different hues which I could mix, but there was another way to achieve different colors and that was by adding oxides or stains," explains Talmath.

The next step, after the floor was dried and polished to a fine patina, was to apply a series of oils and finishes, starting with boiled linseed oil, heated to penetrate the adobe, followed by more coats of oil thinned with mineral liquids. The layers were applied to the point of saturation.

The final step was a coat of hardening oil consisting of a mixture of fruit, nut, and tung oil.

Adobe, straw and clay provide superb insulation for a solar house; the natural materials, and radiant heating from roof to basement and walls to floors combine to create a traditional or modern green home of distinction. (www.greenhomebuilding.com)

Talmath still owns, but no longer works at MudCrafters because, as he said, "The flooring work was so hard on my knees, they gave out one day." But he gives back by teaching his methods. He is also writing a book on adobe techniques. His installation business, New Gen Energy, installs solar hot water heating systems, photovoltaic systems, and wind generators for private clients.

From Yoshihiro Suzuki's clay roof tiles to Talmath Lakai's adobe floors, earthen plasters and clay paints, they cover many aspects of a stunning sustainable house.

MudCrafters
P.O. Box 344
Crestone, CO 81131
Phone: (719) 256-4197
www.mudcrafters.com

NATURAL LIVING

Ho Jai Cheung and Semmania Luk of Hong Kong own three shops called Natural Living. In 2000 they created a company called Ecotec Natural Paint (Ltd.) that sells the brand Ecozmo—natural paint developed and manufactured in Germany. They are the sole distributors in China of Ecozmo. But the company is also a wholesaler—or a form of wholesaler—that amounts to a percentage off retail prices to painters, construction companies and related trades' people.

Ho Jai trained as an architect and Semmania as a graphic artist. Neither had any retail experience. She is their marketing director. She designs and writes all catalogs and brochures; literature that contributes to the education of eco-friendly people and encourages environmental responsibility as well as promotes their products on the Internet.

Ecozmo established tough rules for the products long before it was "fashionable" or even mainstream: ingredients of raw materials had to be biodegradable and raw materials had to be derived from replenishable sources. Their products do not contain chemicals (no longer allowed by environment-conscious governments and health authorities).

Their products are characterized by no VOC (volatile organic compounds), no formaldehyde, no benzene, PVC (polyvinyl chloride)-free.

All of the above are toxic and/or lethal for some people. The paint is also breathable, static free, absorbs pollutants (i.e. smoke) and is allergy free (in comparison to regular paint).

Ho Jai adds that a natural paint system is formulated with non-toxic raw-earth-materials, has a porous structure and the company conforms to international standards for health and safety. Further, claims are the aesthetics are absolutely no different from traditional paints.

The extensive product line of Natural Living includes:

- Mineral Paints

- Eco Emulsion—HKGLS certified—a combination of minerals, plants and water

- Milk Paint—protein-based paint (or casein) powder form mixed with water

- Clay Paint and Products: derived totally from natural clays

- Clay Plaster—a mix of fine sands and clay

- Clay Board—in place of plaster board; absorbs odors and is an effective sound insulator

- Clay Blocks—made from unfired clay and straw; serve as partition walls

- Paint Accessories: 16 colors to create different shades and tinted glazes

- Color Wash—a tinted transparent glaze applied over mineral paints.

- Various tools—rubber stamps, block brush, ragging tool, Veneziano roller, used with combinations of paints to create unusual effects

- Wall Glaze—extra protection and color applied over mineral paints

- Texture Base—mixed with mineral paints to create a variety of rough-textured finishes

- Pigments

- Floor and Wood Finishes

- ❧ PHS Oil—HKGLS certified transparent primer for wood

- ❧ Wood Preserver Primer—protects all woods from molds and insects in damp environments

- ❧ Clear Varnish—maximum protection against sunlight

- ❧ White Undercoat

- ❧ Exterior Gloss—weather-resistant paint

- ❧ Interior Eggshell—water-based washable paint

- ❧ Thinner—made from citrus oils and orange peel leftovers from plantations in Brazil, it is a natural thinner for diluting oil-based paints, cleaning brushes, and paint-stain remover.

- ❧ WBC Wax—HKGLS certified—water-based wax for all painted surfaces; diluted, it is also a cleaner and restorer of wood surfaces.

Hong Kong Green Label Scheme certification, or HKGLS, is the "authoritative, independent and public-acceptable green label." It is awarded by the combined green counsel (GC) and the Hong Kong Productivity Council (HKPC). The process of certification for a product (or company) to be considered 100 percent green is extremely costly, lengthy and time consuming.

Consequently, a company will submit only one or two products at a time to the appropriate certification board. To qualify for the green label products have to be independently assessed and proved to fulfill a series of pre-set environmental requirements. Typically, they involve proving that a product is comprised of topnotch environmental raw materials or ingredients, sustainability factors and protections for people by a group of experts.

In Hong Kong, the group is composed of various academics, industrial and environmental organizations which conduct the analysis. A sampling of the requirements for green paint, in addition to those stated by Ecozmo and Ecotec, include:

    • The paint shall not contain halogenated solvents (in excess of the stated amount)

    • The paint shall not be formulated or manufactured with mercury, arsenic or selenium or their compounds or be tinted with pigment of lead, cadmium, chromium or antimony.

    • Packaging requirements: the paint cans and their components shall not be fabricated with lead.

There are many more intricate requirements as well.

Ecozmo / Ecotec have three HKGLS labels with hopes, in time, for more.

Natural Living also carries a line of silicates. Suitable for protecting, decorating and renovating historical buildings as well as modern structures exterior and interior wall surfaces, silicate paint offers good weather protection and excellent resistance to acid rain. The products are AZ paint, water-repellant paint, light-textured paint, mineral glaze and AZ fixative.

Each of the shops is completely decorated with panels of clay boards covered with examples of combined paints and special effects. One of Ho Jai's goals was to make the shops themselves environmentally sound. As a green architect, he designed his office and workspaces to achieve an optimal green environment. And wonderful and soaring spaces they are.

Both of them, Semmania said, are "dedicated to the greater goal of a pure atmosphere." In fact, so dedicated are the couple to an eco-friendly way of life that they live within a 10-minute walk from their home which is located in an almost bucolic and quiet, hilly area of Hong Kong.

Within five years they hope to expand their shops into other Asian countries while their long-term goal is the creation of franchises worldwide. The business partners, who are married, incorporate as many green principles as possible in their businesses.

The only commercial advertising they feel is profitable is the yellow pages of the phone book. But Ho Jai attends many trade shows, expos and fairs of which Hong Kong has a plethora: Eco Expo, Innovation and Technology, Home Show, Natural Products Expo and, in Tokyo, EIY Show. At all these events, he displays the Ecotec line and finds the shows profitable in terms of meeting potential clients of construction companies and real estate developers.

Ho Jai Cheung and Semmania Luk so believed in their green product, natural paint, that they started their business with only savings. After all, does not almost every home and business in every country worldwide use paint?

Natural Living
8/F, Sungib Industrial Centre
53 Wong Chuk Hang Road
Aberdeen, Hong Kong
Phone: (852) 2847-3377
Fax: (852) 2868-5233
www.naturalliving.hk

FERGUSON

In 2008, the U.S. Environmental Protection Agency honored Ferguson as the first Retail and Distributor WaterSense Partner of the Year. Ferguson earned this distinction for promoting water-efficiency awareness. WaterSense—a partnership program the EPA launched in 2006—seeks to protect the future of the nation's water supply by offering people simple ways to use less water.

The Ferguson chain started in 1953 with $150,000 and two locations. Plumbing has always been its core business; today, it's the largest plumbing wholesaler in North America. In 1982, Ferguson was sold to U.K.-based Wolseley PLC, which finances Ferguson as it doubles in size every five years through expansion into the industrial, heating and cooling (HVAC) and waterworks market. It is the second-largest distributor of these products in addition to pipes, valves and fittings.

Ferguson now has more than 400 showrooms-turned-retail-stores and more than 4,000 wholesale outlets for contractors and architects in the United States alone. The outlets are there for "inner" or mechanical works—plumbing, pipes, valves and fittings, waterworks, heating and cooling—while the retail operations are the "outer" side. The retail showrooms offer appliances, kitchen sinks, tubs/showers, toilets and seats, bath and kitchen fixtures, cabinets and furniture, decorative lighting, ceiling and bathroom exhaust fans, lighting and fan accessories, home amenities, bathroom accessories, medicine cabinets, fireplaces and steam units.

In 2005, Tim Morgan—then a 24-year veteran of the heating, plumbing and lighting business—was recruited in 2005 by Ferguson's general manager in Monterey County, California, to run the large Santa Cruz industrial outlet.

In the United States alone, Ferguson has more than 400 showroom-turned-retail stores and more than 4,000 wholesale outlets for contractors and architects.

Architect Safwat Malek introduced me to Tim in a showplace retail showroom in Seaside, California "He is one of the most knowledgeable people I know in the business and is completely devoted to customer service," Safwat intoned.

According to Tim, "Green is a top priority for Ferguson because the company knows that the country is going green. So one of its goals is to be number one in its diverse markets. Only about 30 to 35 percent of retail showroom products are green, but they are the greenest products being manufactured in the world. We sell all the green products, including the most advanced in the industry."

Senior executives attend trade shows worldwide. Additionally, most employees involved in retail or wholesale distributor sites are encouraged to attend local trade shows, seeking new products. Wherever a large resource sells, whether big-city showroom or small-town outlet, that manufacturer will likely have representation. Tech-wise, the latest fixtures in the world become available first on the East Coast followed by West Coast locations.

However, not all products are represented in all locations; what moves in a New York store may not be appropriate in a smaller location. At Ferguson, 65 percent of inventory must be carried in all branches. Twenty percent can vary from location to location.

Ferguson enlists some of the brightest college and university graduates from around the country through its vigorous recruiting program. Branch managers recruit locally for salespeople familiar with local needs. It employs about 17,000 people nationwide, with a network of about 1,350 service centers in Puerto Rico, Colombia, the Caribbean and Mexico.

Several years back, when Ferguson added retail stores, it made service its top priority, requiring all employees to take a one-year online customer service course by Jeffrey Gitomer, and sends some employees to schools that teach the difference between selling to contractors and to consumers.

Tim notes that Germany is number one in the world in green manufacturing, and is "15 to 20 years ahead of the United States. That country has led in technology for two reasons," he said. "The German people are aware and concerned about the environment, and they are the most technologically minded people in Europe."

Switzerland and France are in the same category, but they are smaller countries that do not want to expand and hence prefer not to export their goods. A few other countries produce items that contribute to the 50 percent European output. Ferguson carries two lighting resources and six plumbing, appliance and fixtures companies from Germany alone.

European kitchens and bathrooms in apartments, condos, and average houses are much smaller than in the United States. "In Europe, everything is condensed," Tim reminds. "Therefore, fixtures are smaller and more efficient." For example, showers, toilets, sinks and "on-demand" water heaters may hang on walls.

"Tubs are narrower but have depth, so they take up less space and need less water," Tim continues. "Toilets are 'high performance' with a gravity flush—meaning they flush immediately and precisely. Because of the system technology, they conserve much more water than one realizes."

Shower columns also conserve water. All controls attach to a panel that hangs on a wall, with no pipes and low flow; water flows directly from the showerhead via an inner line connected to the nearest water pipe.

Appliances such as washing machines conserve 50 percent more water and energy. Clothes set on a rack in a front loader that makes only a one-half turn. "Technically, the machine senses how much water is needed," Tim explained. "Therefore, clothes come out drier, needing less time in the drier, again conserving energy."

The popularity of induction cooktops reflects consumer awareness of green efficiency. Ranges consume much less electricity than other kinds. Underneath a glass cooktop are electric magnets. When a pot or pan with magnetic bottom is placed on a unit, the cooktop heats instantly, cooking food rapidly through the pot bottom only (without any side heating).

It turns itself off instantly when a sensor recognizes food is finished. Digital ovens employ the same induction principles as glass cooktops.

Electronic faucets and the latest water fixtures regulate themselves with an internal metering device that starts and stops with the movement of hands.

In the United States, Kohler is the number one designer of plumbing appliances, fixtures and electric generators. Owner Herb Kohler and his sons have been green-minded for many years. Their fixture and appliance parts are hand-assembled and every bit of iron—used in bathtubs and sinks, for instance—is recycled from sources nationwide.

Ferguson Bath and Kitchen retail showrooms represent the products and manufacturers listed below. Many of these brands have earned Energy Star certification, and/or are LEED qualified and/or have earned certification as green manufacturers.

Ferguson makes an effort to carry the most current, most energy-efficient products available.

Appliances

Bathroom Exhaust Fans

Ceiling Fans

Decorative Lighting

Faucets—Bar, bidet, kitchen, lavatory, tubs, showers

Fixtures—Bath, toilets, sinks, lavatories, bidets, urinals

Bath Furniture

Kitchen Sinks

Medicine Cabinets

Specialty Consoles & Sinks

Tub/shower combinations

Toilet Seats

Whirlpools

Heating & Cooling

Home Amenities—Disposals, ventilation systems

Insulation

Lighting and Fan Accessories

Wall Controls

Steam Units

Water Heaters

On-Demand Water Heaters

∽

Ferguson policy requires managers and salespeople to participate in their communities, joining organizations that interest them: civic, cultural, sports, home building, charity, lecturers, educational and environmental activities.

On a national scale, the company teamed with Habitat for Humanity to build 20 houses for victims of the 2008 floods in Cedar Rapids, Iowa. Ferguson provided toilets and lighting fixtures for the family rooms, kitchens and bathrooms. Every year, the company provides at least two toilets for every house built by Habitat for Humanity anyplace in the United States.

∽

There are so many peripheral aspects of construction that they often spill into other areas, creating new products and business ideas. There are innumerable essential items such as window, door and cabinet hardware—hinges, handles, pulls, latches, and door knobs—as well as hand rails, doorbells, light switches, grates, thermostats, and even recyclable smoke alarms. There are cleaning products for floors, walls and other surfaces made of natural materials like bamboo, hemp, cork and stone. Ferguson, which seeks to become as green as possible for both business and personal reasons, is one of the most successful in leading the green trend.

Ferguson
1144 Fremont Blvd.
Seaside, CA 93955
Phone: (831) 394-7469
www.ferguson.com

CHAPTER 7

HOME, GARDEN AND OFFICE

The array of products available for homes, gardens and offices includes not only furniture, but also products in myriad categories such as tools, garden supplies, indoor and outdoor cleaning supplies, lamps, paintings, books, window treatments and kitchen ware, as well as and all sorts of gift items for adults and children. The categories are almost endless.

The three stores presented here—Green Depot, Environment Furniture and GreenSky—are examples of home, garden and office furnishings stores and showrooms that not only sell products for interiors and exteriors, but also established, and continue to operate, their businesses in a green way. They agreed to share their secrets with you, the potential green business owner.

GREEN DEPOT

In 2005, Green Depot was born. The company—a large, green-as-can-possibly-be purveyor of building materials for contractors—started as a construction-trade business and evolved into an outstanding retailer. Based in the Northeast, it has a flagship store in the Bowery section of New York City, eight other retail locations, and 10 distribution centers.

The renovated 3,500-square-foot historical landmark building, constructed in 1885 as the first YMCA in New York, houses the retail store.

Sarah Beatty, a Harvard graduate, founded Green Depot and remains its president. In 2001, Sarah—then senior vice president of the marketing and creative divisions of USA Network (and 10-year veteran of MTV, where she was vice president of trade marketing and global branding) —was only vaguely aware of the burgeoning environmentally friendly world.

A few years later, pregnant with her first child, she recognized that the green building trend was real. She was searching for eco-friendly products for her apartment renovations, which included a new nursery, and became frustrated by the lack of availability of paints, finishes and furnishings that reduced toxins and volatile organic compounds. She ultimately parlayed her concerns about her baby and interest in safer products for the home into a retail store.

The 3,500-square-foot building where the store opened has a remarkable history. It was constructed in 1885 (as the first YMCA in New York. In 1940, artist Fernand Leger rented studio space upstairs, as did artist Mark Rothko, who painted Seagram murals on the walls in 1959. In 1998, the building at 222 Bowery was granted historical landmark status by the Landmarks Commission of New York City. It was not necessary for Green Depot to do this because they are tenants, not owners, but they wanted to protect the historical status of the building. Ten years later, the company leased the ground floor and renovated it as a LEED Platinum-certified commercial interior space. (LEED stands for Leadership in Energy and Environment Design, the U.S. Green Building Council's green rating program for buildings.) In the renovation, she would always keep in mind the four R's:

- Reused—the original maple "gymnasium" floor

- Recycled—building elements refurbished into sculptural pieces from salvaged steel, water heaters and cast iron water tables

- Renewed—original wood trim and bricks (that survived a fire)

- Repurposed—exposed original tile that outlined the location of the 1915 YMCA swimming pool

The renovations included restrooms built with Green Depot products, including woven bamboo flooring.

On entry, it feels like a large, old-time hardware store, but on closer inspection—from displays to products—the store could not be more modern, with educational materials that explain the CLEAR icon system and show how to use products.

Sarah refers to the store, which opened in February 2009, as "a living testament to possibilities for green building and design, demonstrating high quality, high performance green materials."

The store also has an assortment of one-of-a-kind products—vintage and salvaged items and historical objects found during renovations. The aptly named "Found" section undoubtedly would not be found in a typical hardware store.

And where would a baby department be found in such a store?

Paul Novack, Green Depot's in-house expert on environmental health and nontoxic construction materials, works closely with medical professionals and environmental scientists to help create nontoxic environments. With 30 years of resourcing, defining and selling eco-friendly building products—and as the founder of Environmental Construction Outfitters of New York, one of the oldest environmental building companies in the country—he has the experience to consult with customers, architects and builders. He represents the company at consumer and trade shows, including Green Build, New Jersey Holistic Medical Show, Speck It Green, New York City Green Building Show, Urban Green Building Show and the New York Green Home Show.

From the beginning, the company instituted two concepts: systems and services. Of the systems, the first—Green Depot Filter—is a proprietary chemicals management system (CMS) that defines the company's standards, is used as an employee-training tool and ensures quality control. "As a green retailer developing an internal CMS it is vital to understand firsthand the role that chemicals play in the products we sell," Sarah says.

She works with in-house experts, Paul and Jenny Gitlitz, and an outside consultant to define green products for retailing purposes and determine criteria for evaluating products. The purpose is to educate consumers. The acronym CLEAR encompasses the categories of green products:

- C—Conservation

- L – Local

- E – Energy

- A – Air Quality

- R – Responsibility

Conservation involves certification third party, such as the Forest Stewardship Council, which verifies wood removed from sustainable forests. Green Depot's conservation-oriented products for water include The Sprite shower filter, which eliminates chlorine and other harmful substances from water; Casabella Oxygenics Tri Spa low-flow showerhead; Casabella cleaning accessories (made exclusively for Green Depot), which are devoid of toxic material and chemicals; and Caroma's dual-flush toilets, small flush and larger flush, a breakthrough in water-saving technology. Other products born of conservation include Umbra Frosine glasses, reclaimed from Goodwill and recycled as frosted glasses; and glass tumblers recycled from wine bottles. Greed Depot's nontoxic soy or beeswax candles last much longer than regular paraffin wax made from crude oil.

Local products can be found near where they are manufactured, such as vintage bathroom fixtures salvaged from recycle centers and retrofitted with water-saving devices. Local artisans' furniture and housewares are Green Depot Designer Exclusives. Ivy Coatings' zero-VOC paints are manufactured in Brooklyn, but they can custom mix or match a sample using its optical scanner.

Energy can be reduced with these products: compact fluorescent light bulbs, which use 75 percent less energy than incandescent bulbs; power strips for entertainment systems and computers (they save energy especially when electronics are plugged in but not turned on); and Solatube, a tubular skylight and ventilation kits that reduces moisture.

Air quality improves with Solatube's Ventilation Kit. Powered by the sun, it allows free flow of fresh air and prevents mold buildup. GD Cleaning formulas, made in New York, are nonhazardous.

Responsibility begins with purchasing decisions. Consider Green Depot area rugs, available in wool, silk, jute, hemp, and sisal in plain and patterned designs and in different sizes (RugMark-certified and Fair Trade); Vessell's separate recyclables bin system; Nature Mill Plus composter; Cascade Worm Factory, a worm compost system; RSVP stainless steel and RSVP stonewear compost pails.

Every product available at Green Depot must fit into one of the CLEAR categories: halftones designate better-than-conventional products but have room for improvement, and full tones designate whether they meet or exceed the company's own standards (which are LEED standards).

This system reveals the products that are indisputably green and not green washed—"a term used [by Green Depot] to describe exaggerated, misleading, or inaccurate statements by a company regarding the environmental benefits of a product, service or the environmental practices of the company." An example of green washing: "calling materials green when the materials are harmful to humans and the environment," Sarah explains.

To meet Green Depot's standard, manufacturers must answer an in-depth questionnaire and provide all of the product's spec sheets, Material Safety Data Sheets, test results from independent laboratories and third-party certifications.

The company's 'green filter team' then compares those with its own specifications, based on EPA toxic-chemical lists; the State of California, which exceeds EPA standards with more regulated chemicals; and the nonprofit Environmental Defense Fund, which determines whether the manufacture should provide more information. It is with this stringent system that they feel protected from false claims and green washing.

The Green Depot Filter System has many benefits, especially protecting businesses from liability. But Green Depot has faced significant challenges, such as limited information about chemical composition from suppliers that often claim the information is proprietary. The business requires extensive (and costly) research into potential "red flag" chemicals. Another challenge is customer confusion about green washing.

The store also developed services, which are in two parts. The first is actual services—one of which, Flip It Green, helps customers directly. For instance, a customer with conventional architectural blueprints for a new house or renovation can learn how to incorporate green specifications with local products and materials. As a retailer, Sarah believes more and more consumers not only expect detailed information about products, but also transparency about every aspect of the store.

Another service, the 360 Network, is for green building professionals. The purpose is to form groups, located near each Green Depot retail location, to network for referrals to projects.

Service also includes displays, such as the Light Booth made of recycled acrylic material; a walk-in booth, which allows customers to test different types of light bulbs or to view paint chips and color options under different lighting conditions.

Last is the recycling service. Customers can return CFL bulbs purchased from the store's recycling center and unused portions of Ivy Coatings paints purchased at Green Depot (which ships the leftover to the Ivy Coatings factory for use in the manufacture of a recycled paint line).

Perhaps the most unusual aspect of the store is located just inside the entrance: The GD Cleaning Station, which features 5-gallon recyclable plastic jugs containing the company's locally made liquid cleaning supplies. A customer who buys a regular size of one or more of GD cleaning products can bring the container back for refill, thereby saving the cost of another bottle. The five plant-based, allergen-free, biodegradable products include dish cleaner, glass and window cleaner, tub and tile cleaner, all-purpose cleaner and fragrance-free all-purpose cleaner.

Green Depot Baby is certainly Sarah's baby. She created it for health. "An environmental health scare when I was pregnant is what drove me to start Green Depot," she says. "Newborns are the most vulnerable to environmental conditions, and preparing for a baby becomes the entry point for understanding what green means and why these practices are important."

Green Depot Baby products are divided into five categories: Home Care, Lifestyle, Design, Build, and Baby. Each is divided into sections, listed below, influencing the store layout.

HOME CARE

Green Depot, Hypoallergenic & Heavy Duty Cleaning

Cleaning Tools, Accessories and Vacuums

Air/Water Filtration & Conservation

Energy & Lighting, including: CFL & LED Light Bulbs & Incandescent Light Bulbs

Recycling Systems, Bags, Liners & Compost

Safety Supplies

Pest Control

Do-It-Yourself (DIY) Toolbox

LIFESTYLE

Green Depot "Found"

Tabletop & Gifts

Home Accessories

Gadgets, Power Strips, Monitors, Lights & Chargers

On-the-Go

Books, including: Baby, Design, DIY & Reference Books

Stationery & Supplies

Kits

DESIGN

Green Depot Designer Exclusives

Green Depot Rug Collection

Cabinets & Countertops

Paints & Finishes, including: Green Depot Color Collections, Ivy Coatings, YOLO Colorhouse, Safecoat Paints & Stains

Paint Accessories, Coatings & Sealants, Strippers

Lamps & Light Fixtures

Flooring

BUILD

Paints, Finishes & Coatings

Flooring

Insulation

Heating & Cooling

Framing, Decking & Molding

Soundproofing

Ceilings & Walls

Roofing & Siding

Adhesives, Caulks & Sealants

Daylighting

BABY

Green Depot Baby

Build-a-Nursery

Furniture & Bedding

Apparel

Baby Gifts & Gear

Baby Safety

❦

The Build sector features several interesting products:

- ❧ Blue Jeans insulation is just that: recycled blue jeans

- ❧ Countertops with quartz surfaces made from recycled glass that results in iridescent tops

- ❧ Counters constructed of bamboo butcher block

- ❧ Flooring manufactured from sustainable materials such as bamboo, cork and natural linoleum (composed of linseed oil derived from the flax plant, wood flour obtained from lumber waste, resins from pine trees, backed with jute fiber)

- ❧ Recycled-glass flooring

One company manufactures an acoustical underlay from 90 percent recycled tires. Another division of this company produces drywall that reduces noise by 70 to 97 percent. Green Depot has its own brand of foundations consisting of bamboo or rare woods from Brazil or Honduras, including Brazilian cherry and white tigerwood, all sustainable.

❦

Earth Day New York and the Natural Resources Defense Council awarded Green Depot its 2009 Business Leader of the Year Award.

❦

Sarah advises entrepreneurs to:

- ❧ define and devise a practical sustainability plan for their business

- ❧ design purchasing, operations and marketing criteria to correspond to that plan

- ❧ be honest when speaking about the green characteristics of their business and the products it sells

- ❧ avoid overstating the green benefits

Green Depot has become a one-stop shop for green building materials, products and services. With its historically renovated building and sharp layout and decor, this 100 percent green operation sets a superb example for other businesses.

Green Depot
222 Bowery
New York, NY 10012
Telephone: (212) 226-0444
contactus@greendepot.com
www.greendepot.com

ENVIRONMENT FURNITURE

Exciting is a word to describe Environment Furniture. Unusual is another. Sophisticated and elegant are appropriate, too, when describing design aesthetics. Combining uncommon woods and textiles, pieces are placed horizontally or vertically depending on their use and available space. An example is a piece that when placed horizontally makes a fine console, and when installed vertically becomes a modern-styled room divider or bookcase.

Giovanni Gallizio and CEO Davide Berruto co-own Environment Furniture, headquartered in Los Angeles, where it has a showroom, a branch in Las Vegas, and a 4,000-square-foot showroom and retail store in New York City that, in addition to furniture—armoires, beds, benches, buffets, chairs, coffee tables, dressers, media consoles, mirrors and occasional tables—offers upholstery bedding, rugs and lighting.

Environment Furniture has a substantial supply of Peroba Rosa, a native Brazilian hardwood and the primary component of the company's furniture. Reclaimed from uninhabitable houses, barns and abandoned buildings in Parana, Brazil, the wood combines with Indonesian mahogany and certified North American hardwoods, such as white oak and poplar. The Sustainable Forestry Initiative (SFI) certifies the latter woods in a program the United Nations Conference on Environment and Development established in 1992 to prevent illegal logging and other environmental-encroachment activities in developing countries.

An independent, nonprofit organization, SFI is internationally recognized as the largest single forest standard in the world. The SFI 2010-2014 Standard—based on principles and measures of maintaining, overseeing and improving forests—promotes sustainable forest management on all U.S. forestlands. Its prestigious logo appears on paper reams, packaging, and two-by-fours.

To ensure its Indonesian mahogany supply contains no illegal or unknown wood, Environment Furniture joined Tropical Forest Trust, a Britain-based nonprofit organization that monitors illegal logging. The trust acts as an intermediary between its members, retailers and manufacturers or suppliers of tropical woods and legal forest management groups.

A signature piece, the Santomer Dining Table is made from Brazilian Peroba Rosa reclaimed from an old coffee factory.

David Putzel, manager of product development and quality control at Environment Furniture, explains that the company seeks "reclaimed or recycled woods closer to home."

The company's marketing director, Camilla Trigano, notes that "The utilization of veneers instead of solid wood refers to thin slices of wood, usually thinner than 1/8 inch, and typically glued onto core panels using particle board, wood board or fiberboard as parts of furniture."

David adds that "wood fiber, plywood chipboard, and flake board are natural fiber wood pulp-based products; wood fiber itself is made from sawdust or wood chips extracted from all parts of trees. Veneers are certified." He also says that Environment Furniture has eliminated all VOC-emitting stains from the production process in favor of naturally derived plant-based dyes.

Another component of furniture manufacturing includes glue which is water-based and needs no additional formaldehyde for bonding. In addition to glue, other water-based products include a wood finish (lacquer) from Saverlack's HydroPlus line, awarded the European Union's Ecolabel certification from independent experts who "verify that they meet rigorous environmental and performance-related criteria."

The California Air Resources Board Air Toxic Control Measures set the standard for reducing formaldehyde gas emissions for composite panels (such as plywood and chipboard) and products that incorporate panels into their furniture construction. The standards, which went into effect on January 1, 2009, could eventually eliminate formaldehyde completely to minimize the carbon footprint.

"Other states must follow suit or face fines," David declares. Federal regulators have spent much time developing a formaldehyde measure, but no measure passed into law as of this writing.

Fabrics that Environment Furniture uses for certain types of chairs are reclaimed tent canvas, linen and organic leathers.

In 2007, the company issued a green operations guide for corporate offices and retail operations. It covers small and large measures, such as application of green design principles, future furniture construction, as well as usage of third-party recycling companies for packaging materials—corrugated cardboard, made from tree pulp and Styrofoam, a recyclable petrochemical-based product.

Although Environment Furniture pieces assert a contemporary design—sleek and sophisticated—their simplicity distinguishes them. An example is a low rectangular occasional table using a small block of contrasting wood for one leg and a narrow piece of wrought iron-like metal encasing the opposite side for the other.

In fact, most of these smartly designed furnishings incorporate elements that suggest tradition. Combinations of designs and materials seem boundless and often produce stunning effects.

Environment Furniture
8126 Beverly Blvd.
Los Angeles, CA 90048
Phone: (323) 935-1330
www.environmentfurniture.com

GREEN SKY

Housed in a large, restored, eco-friendly jewel of a building—at one time a Victorian residence, now shops and apartments—GreenSky is a delightful green, artsy craftsy gift shop of several rooms with a first-floor, side-street entrance.

Nadeen Kieren, GreenSky's proprietor, and her husband, architect Thom Greene, founded Green Sky Company in 2001. In 2006, Nadeen opened the sister enterprise, GreenSky, within the newly restored Victorian, to establish a retail operation—which can be called a gift shop because it offers many different kinds of items—in the heart of Andersonville, a village-like section of Chicago. Though the 1898 Victorian, the oldest commercial building in this section of Chicago, is not 100 percent green, Thom maintained 95 percent of its exterior character using eco-friendly building materials. The interior was restored by converting the original rear apartment/office complex into the shop, GreenSky.

Thom explained that they renovated what they could afford and will incorporate additional green elements into the interior as funds become available. The restoration thus far includes:

- Entry decking made from recycled milk bottles and other reused/recycled materials to create a new entry

- Energy efficiency, historically correct wood windows installed throughout the building

- Reused and low VOC paints

- Fluorescent/LED light bulbs with photo sensors for exterior lighting control

- Ceiling fans throughout instead of air conditioning

- High-reflective roofing to keep sun's rays from further heating the interior in summer

- Programmable thermostats

- Display furniture purchased from local resale shop, a nonprofit where all funds are donated to the local AIDS foundation

- Energy Star-rated appliances

Thom and Nadeen named their company after the missionary Peter Greensky, who built a now-historic log church in the 1840s where they were married.

Interior décor of GreenSky, within the restored Victorian.

A retailer with no prior experience, Nadeen graduated college with an engineering degree but was in the corporate world for more than 20 years. During that time, she was involved in research and development—specifically, converting raw materials of food, such as oils, fats and sugar into finished products.

Thom founded Greene & Proppe Design, which is dedicated to the "art of architecture" and interior design. In

2010, Thom was featured on a Planet Green television program called World's Greenest Homes, which showcased one of the residences he designed and built 100 percent green.

At GreenSky, Nadeen concentrates on two areas. The first is local artists and products; the other is Fair Trade items. She samples items, such as lamps and vases made from Lake Superior rock, book journals made from recycled hardcover books and recycled paper as well as journals created from elephant-pooh paper, wooden cutting boards handmade from virgin wood scraps and recycled glass items—sun catchers (a decorative hanger strand of colorful glass pieces), bottle stoppers, and green glassware derived from reclaimed wine bottles.

The second area of products Nadeen feels particularly strongly about is Fair Trade items like handbags, wallets and coin purses made from inner tube tires and plastic trash bags collected from trash bins; Balinese suar wood sculptures; scarves fashioned from reclaimed T-shirts and knit throws derived from reclaimed knitting machine discards. The Wisconsin company, which actively employs disabled people, also repurposes rain barrels and composters made from reclaimed barrels originally used to import foods like olives. These are among the 200 products Nadeen carries in four categories: kitchen and bath, house and garden, decorative art, and handbags and jewelry

Among the house and garden products are Polywood chairs for garden, beach or terrace that come in six colors which make a startling display at GreenSky. In 2010, Nadeen said customers were buying color-matched tables, ottomans, gliders and rockers from the collection catalog because her shop, while large, is too small to display all the samples. What makes these products unique is they are made from recycled plastic milk jugs—500 jugs per chair.

One of the Fair Trade items she sells is chocolate bars. The first Fair Trade chocolate company in Ghana, Kuapa Kokoo, a farmers' cooperative of 45,000 members, supplies the cocoa beans and are co-owners of Divine Chocolate. They receive a guaranteed Fair Trade price for the beans and a "social premium," or investment, in their schools, medical clinics, clean water and women's entrepreneurship projects, such as the production of batik and soap. As co-owners they have a share in the profits and a say in the company.

Nadeen's best selling, most popular items are:

- Bamboo handbags
- Inner tube tire handbags
- Car license plate art
- Birdhouses
- French soap
- 100 percent eco-friendly, green glassware
- Bamboo/organic cotton towels in three sizes and a variety of colors

GreenSky is open Thursdays to Sundays, and Wednesdays from mid-October through December. Nadeen is the sole salesperson except for a friend who helps out on occasion. "When business and the economy pick up I will be able to hire staff six days a week," she declares.

For now, she has another business Mondays through Wednesdays "to pay the bills." In business, she moves slowly and methodically because, she believes, one reason that businesses fail is "they grow too big, too fast without the right infrastructure in place, and then they implode."

She and Thom attend the Philadelphia Buyers Market, Beckmans' Handcrafted Market, Chicago Art Fair and Chicago/Seattle Green Fest as buyers. They sell products at the Andersonville Midsommerfest Fair, which Nadeen says is somewhat successful in sales but very successful for exposure.

They also attend art fairs—Royal Oak Clay & Glass Festival, Old Town Art Fair, Bucktown Art Fair and Frankfort Art Fair—which are small, independent and local fairs, composed of cottage industries. The artists and craftspeople work mostly out of their houses and garages, collecting many of the raw materials from alleys and dumpsters.

Nadeen has a website, but not an online retail store; however, that's in the works. GreenSky also has exposure via artist/craftsman's' websites.

She relies on four neighborhood newsletters for advertising and also the Chamber of Commerce e-mail blasts, her own e-mail list and e-zine (a periodical e-mail blast to her mailing list with sales, events and promotion news) because she caters mostly to locals.

In addition, she has established a tradition of open houses—especially during holidays—where she highlights Andersonville's local not-for-profit products. The arts and crafts people explain their mission and the purpose of their products; Nadeen gives discounts to customers for such purchases on that day. For example, on July 4, 2010, rain barrel and composting demonstrations were featured because Chicago is encouraging people to conserve water and reduce waste. Under the city's rebate program, customers could send in a form and receive a $30 rebate for a rain barrel, above and beyond GreenSky's discount. The city estimates up to 40 percent of household water use can be saved during the summer. The (current) mayor is supports "green" and beautification through trees, flowers and gardens, Nadeen explains. Hence, he created incentives by encouraging people to recapture water and create compost for gardens.

The rain barrels and composters Nadeen sells are repurposed food barrels made by a for-profit company outside of Chicago. According to Nadeen, 700,000 to 900,000 food barrels enter the United States every year, with 75 percent discarded into landfills.

The previous month, she selected the increasingly popular Polywood outdoor furniture from the South Beach Collection at a 15 percent discount as a special one-time offer. It is quite an investment for GreenSky, but Nadeen's customers have multiplied as a result and have become repeat customers purchasing other items as well.

Thom and Nadeen used their own savings exclusively for the start-up inventory. GreenSky has paid back those "loans" and has no other debt; it pays for all merchandise up front or within 30 days of delivery.

At the end of 2008, Nadeen projected a 30 percent increase for 2009, but due to the recession, her increase was only 8 percent; however, six months into 2010, she was already 39 percent ahead.

Nadeen relates this story:

"I carry a line of handbags made of bamboo by a Fair Trade company. A customer was looking at them, inside and out, as she should. She picked up a red one, opened it up and found a rather large fish skeleton inside the bag! We all had a laugh (though I was horrified). Needless to say, the customer did not buy the bag. Lesson learned; open and inspect every item before it gets on the floor!"

GreenSky is a work in progress. The Victorian building is now a local architectural award winner in a neighborhood that in May 2010 was designated as a National Commercial Historic District. GreenSky has recently been accepted into Co-Op America, as it is Andersonville's first certified green business.

GreenSky
5357 N. Ashland Ave.
Chicago, IL 60640
Phone: 773-275-1911
Fax: 773-334-1911
www.greenskycompany.com

CHAPTER 8

ORGANIC FOOD

Organic, as defined by the Organic Trade Association refers to how agricultural products—food and fiber (cotton, linen, flax)—are grown and processed. Organic food production is based on a farming system that maintains soil fertility without use of toxic pesticides or fertilizers—and delivered with no artificial ingredients, preservatives or irradiation.

Organic foods are proliferating year by year. They include beer, breads, cereals, cheeses, chocolate, cookies and cakes, frozen juices, frozen meals, ice cream novelties, ice cream, meats and poultry, milk, pastas, soups, wines, and vodka.

Inadvertently, organic crops are exposed to agricultural chemicals in rain and ground water via wind and rain drifts. Therefore, a certifier may permit a farmer to apply botanicals derived from plants and broken down by oxygen and sunlight.

U.S. sales of organic food and beverages have grown from $1 billion in 1990 to $23.6 billion in 2008, the last figure report, after which it is projected to grow an average of 18 percent per annum until now. (©2008, Organic Trade Association, www.ota.com)

FARMERS MARKETS

California is referred to as the "salad bowl of America," and is generally considered the organic produce and fruit crops capital of the United States. As such, alternative, as well as typical, venues exist for selling its products that might be unavailable in other parts of the country—even though organic farming is taking hold in most of states.

People are most familiar with farmers markets. Approximately 5,000 farmers markets do business in the United States (600 in California alone), although many countries are even more familiar with them. The U.S. Department of Agriculture publishes a Farmers Market directory.

The list of products available vary in different locales, but in California, the basic items vary little from north to south and east to west:

- Vegetables (seasonal)—artichokes, lettuce, potatoes, carrots, beets, onions, cabbage, chard and many more varieties.

- Fruits—strawberries, melons, cherries, apples, apricots, plums, tomatoes, peaches, pears, oranges, tropical fruits, bananas, all kinds of berries and varieties of most fruits

- Whole grain breads

- Cooking oils, olive oils (varieties)

- Jams and jellies

- Cheeses

- Honey

- Herbs

- Baskets

- Chocolate

- Nuts

- Potted plants and flowers; and cut flowers

- Hand-crafted items

From Beverly Hills to San Diego, San Francisco to points east, north and south, California farmers markets unfold once, twice, three times a week; some cities even have daily markets. Every state has farmers markets.

FAIR TRADE FOOD

Who would think to connect supermarkets and Fair Trade? Green America. It links Fair Trade advocates with stores in their communities and pressures supermarkets to carry Fair Trade products. A few such markets already carry about a half dozen items today.

In 2006, the Green America Adopt-a-Supermarket Campaign's more that 250 teams 'adopted' supermarkets around the United States. No new teams are operating today; rather, Green America publishes the how-to's of forming a team in its Adopt-a-Supermarket Campaign Guide. Teams can approach supermarket managers with Fair Trade products such as sugar, rice, tea, coffee, vanilla, bananas, wine and olive oil.

In this country, Fair Trade food products carry the label of the certifying body, TransFair USA. (www.transfairusa.org).

Consumers can find the extensive list of Fair Trade retailers, wholesalers and producers at Green America (www.greenamerica.org).

THE FARMER AND THE COOK

Olivia Chase and Steve Sprinkel own an intriguing and delightful three-part business in Meiners Oaks, California. The area encompassing Ventura, Carpinteria, Ojai, and other nearby towns is considered by many the organic farming center of Southern California—including celebrities from Hollywood and high-echelon business executives who live in Ojai. Steve and Olivia, husband and wife, live there because they want to be surrounded by the organic food lifestyle. So it is with Olivia Chase, the cook, and Steve Sprinkel, the farmer, who own an aptly-named Ojai business: The Farmer and The Cook. The three parts of the organic food operation include Steve's farm and Olivia's market with a bakery and an indoor/outdoor café. They own The Farmer and The Cook jointly but have their own areas of concentration—as the name implies.

Their story, both personal and business, is fascinating.

Olivia, a trained nutritionist, in the years between 1979 and 1988 received a Bachelor of Science degree in nutrition and foods, a Masters degree in nutrition from the University of Washington, Seattle, and worked as a nutritionist in San Francisco. She found she "did not like trying to persuade people to eat vegetables and whole grains;" she really did not like teaching.

She returned to Ventura in Southern California in 1986 where she opened the City Bakery-Cafe in 1988 while studying for her Masters.

Olivia started her business with $7,000; needing more, she maxed out two credit cards. A friend then invested $5,000 but needing still more, her father lent her $10,000. It amounted to about $30,000 in all.

She started out by doing all the cooking and baking herself, but as business flourished, she hired employees to help her with those tasks. She had learned the basics of cooking as part of the curriculum for her BS degree but had learned to bake all kinds of bread in high school as a 'rebellious vegetarian', she said. Over the years, she took specialized cooking classes by the day in Los Angeles and weeklong classes in London and Paris while pursuing her degrees. She has, she said, learned more from traveling and eating than from cookbooks.

When Olivia opened the Ventura business in 1988, she immediately placed an ad in the local city paper but that was the extent of her advertising. She participated in annual street fairs and festivals in Santa Barbara and Ojai as the first approach to her marketing where she sold several different types of food and baked goods.

Other types of marketing included catering the main meals at various retreats in the area which tended to be two or three day events. The first one was a yoga retreat—she and her son handed out coupons to young mothers in the parking lot of her son's school and donated gift certificates to school fundraising auctions, which of course targeted the very people she wanted to reach: young couples, singles, kids and families. She did this for four years, until 1992, after which she was so busy that she eliminated everything except gift certificates.

During this period of time, Olivia met Steve. In 1989 she was purchasing vegetables at the farmer's market in Ojai for her bakery-cafe, asking questions of the farmer who was selling them, thought him particularly knowledgeable, left, and forgot about him. A decade later, in 1999, she met him again, in the same place, wound up talking with him for hours after the market closed, during which time she discovered four things: that they both held the same views, had the same goals, felt passionate about what each was doing and she and Steve were falling in love.

A year earlier, she had sold her Ventura business and she and Steve started making plans to open a business of their own—a cafe and a market where Steve would supply his vegetables—which they would own jointly.

Olivia and Steve opened The Farmer and The Cook in 2001. They were married in August 2003.

ॐ

Steve, a farmer, describes himself as "a loving son of one of Southern California's most prominent highway builders," slated to step into his father's shoes, was sent one day to survey an orange orchard for a soon-to-be built road. "Standing there," Steve said, looking at the orange trees, "I knew I could not follow in my father's footsteps."

He had studied art at University of California at Santa Barbara and begun gardening in an empty lot next door to his apartment. From Santa Barbara he moved to Oahu, Hawaii, where he learned to farm for a living. He leased farms in Texas and elsewhere prior to leasing 12 acres of land in Ojai from the county. The land had been the site of a minimum security prison until 10 years previously. With the help of one full-time employee and 10 regular volunteers, he worked the land with two tractors. Since then, Steve has been forced to move his farm five times due to the development of the valuable land on which he was farming.

Steve is also a writer and an activist. For 10 years, starting in 1997, he has been writing Transitions, a monthly column for Acres USA that has been in circulation for 50 years. During this period, the USDA published the Final Rule, as it was called, on the National Organic Program, while mainstream agriculture entered the era of genetically-modified food and fiber production.

He continues to write a weekly newsletter, The Forager, as part of his farm's CSA program—CSA (Community Supported Agriculture) is an international program that enables individuals to pledge their support to a farmer by committing to the purchase of produce during each growing season. Most are families who buy a weekly share of his vegetable production.

He states, "This ensures a regular income so I can continue farming." He is also a board member of the Cornucopia Institute whose goal is to empower farmers—together with consumers—to produce local organic food. Cornucopia is considered the toughest watchdog agency for protection of the integrity of the organic label, Steve explained.

∞

In 1989 Olivia was buying lettuce, zucchini and tarragon from a farmer named Steve who invited her to see his farm. She remembers standing in the field saying to Steve, "Wouldn't it be great to have a restaurant right on a farm?" They were married to others at the time but she hurried him over to Meiners Oaks, a former 1940's grocery store, and showed him an old wooden walk-in refrigerator. The store was just what she had been looking for—old, with character, in an affordable location with plenty of parking.

They leased the Meiners Oaks building in 2000 which was in such bad shape "you could see the stars through the hole in the ceiling" Olivia continues. They opened in 2001; it had taken eight months to complete food service requirements. But the most important decision was to create and execute the menu: a process of merging their ideas with customer requests.

Steve's commitment to organic farming led them to open an all-organic market. Olivia thought, having been in the restaurant business, food costs would make it very difficult to make a profit with an all-organic menu. Still, she "threw herself" into the business.

In 2001 the organic meat and poultry market was undeveloped, therefore they became an organic vegetarian café with an organic market. Even so, there were still a few products they could not buy because they did not exist, such as organic tarragon, coconut milk, dried chilies and artisanal cheeses. However, these items, along with an increasing number of organic products, appeared during their next 10 years of business.

Fresh farm-grown vegetables are displayed in market baskets.

In the beginning Olivia and Steve wrote a business plan which they recently reread. "The list of 'why not's' [to open the business] is the most interesting," explains Olivia. "Poor location, working class neighborhood, undercapitalized, lack of talented employee pool." But an important decision was to create and execute the menu: a process of merging their ideas with customer requests. A few factors influenced her menu. That was the first factor.

Steve had attended a going-out-of-business restaurant auction to look for tables and chairs. He returned with them, bought at 25 to 50 percent off what new tables and chairs would have cost—plus a free salad bar that took nine men to help load on his truck. Instantly, a salad bar became part of the menu.

The second factor was a decision to introduce one special meal a day: Mondays were tamales; Tuesdays, shitake mushroom sandwiches; Wednesdays, nut loaves; Thursdays, Indian curries; Fridays, pizzas; Saturdays, veggie burgers; Sundays, sourdough pancakes. "The children of our customers woke up their parents asking what day of the week it was by the menu, not the calendar," Olivia notes.

Through this method she discovered that people were more likely to eat vegetarian foods if they resembled popular foods with which they were familiar. Veggie burgers and pizza were the most requested menu items.

The downturn in the economy actually helped The Farmer and The Cook. By 2008, their values had become mainstream.

But early in 2009, Olivia changed the entire menu to a Mexican one. "I don't recommend changing a whole menu," she remarks ruefully. "Customers do not like change." They apologized and gave their customers the recipes for the daily specials. They explained why they needed to change: their food costs were too high. (The formula to price a fare item in the restaurant business is the cost of ingredients plus four times that figure; labor and overhead are approximately 30% each. Profit is, hopefully, 10%.)

Olivia needed to think, she continues, "more like a cook in a third-world country." She was cooking a different meal each day often having to throw away—compost—the leftovers. The most popular time of day was lunchtime but Olivia was serving full meals, as one would for dinner, all day. Customers came in groups and often they did not all want the same meal, so Olivia added veggie burgers to the menu. In addition, Steve could not grow year round many of the ingredients in the recipes she was preparing but he could grow tomatillos, tomatoes and chilies, the basic ingredients of Mexican food which Olivia could combine with other ingredients to create her menus.

At that time she employed a reliable (very important in the restaurant business) crew of Mexican cooks who were consistent and proud to be cooking the foods and recipes they had learned from their mothers.

Furthermore, she could dry the chilies and tomatoes and freeze the tomatillos for the next season's menu. Olivia is the decision-maker concerning seed purchases—based on future menu items and their climatic conditions: very hot summers are perfect for growing tomatoes, beans and peppers.

Together, the changes decreased their costs; savings came from this new cost-efficient menu. The biggest savings came in the form of carrying over a menu selection from one day to the next before composting leftovers.

They also continue take-out sandwiches, soups and, of course, the salad bar.

Recently the menu became completely vegan-friendly. This proves to be a good idea and she resists adding meat to the menu to appeal to a wider customer base. Steve's philosophy of "don't change it if it is already fixed" prevails.

∽

At present the market offers:

- 170 organic dry goods products, including crackers, pastas, cookies, cereals, condiments, oils, vinegars, soy sauce, canned tomatoes, seaweeds, olives, chips, soups, nut butters, honeys, juices, waters, milk alternatives (almond and oat milk), baking ingredients, hemp seed, hemp protein shake powder (3 flavors)

- 48 organic bulk products such as beans, nuts, flours, sugars, dried fruits, extra virgin olive oil, local orange honey, organic maple syrup, organic tamari

- Organic personal care items offered including shampoo, conditioner, lotion, massage oil

- Organic household items including dish soap and laundry soap.

- 15 organic frozen foods—stocked in their two-door freezer: ice cream, Coconut Bliss (dairy-free ice cream), popsicles, bison, local free-range ground beef, salmon, bacon, turkey dogs, breads, tortillas, vegetables, concentrated orange juice, tempeh and veggie burgers (their own and a commercial brand)

- 34 organic cold products in two grab-and-go refrigerators including 12 kinds of cheese, butter, non-dairy butter, sour cream, veganaise, soy milk, milk, half-and-half, soy creamer, yogurt, soy yogurt, kefir, miso, tofu, tofu burgers, yeast, kelp noodles, kombucha, kefira, orange juice, ice tea, hemp oil, flax oil

- 125 bulk herbs and spices

Shoppers love bulk spices because there is such a cost savings. A spice jar of basil in a supermarket holds 1-2 ounces and is pricey but 2 ounces of fresh basil would only cost about only $2 when purchased in bulk. Ingredient sources for all-organic foods are more difficult to find than the non-organic foods found in an ordinary markets. She orders directly from 30 small companies because they are too small to be part of a large distribution chain; they are not worth the trouble to source separately. But she does have two major suppliers for grocery items: United National Foods (UNFI) and Nature's Best.

She orders organic pecans and masa directly from a Texas grower; organic goat cheese from Montana; organic bison from Nebraska, ground free-range beef from a local source. One February she ordered 10 pounds of parmesan cheese online, but the second order, during the summer, "arrived at my doorstep a sweaty mess." Lesson learned.

On a trip to San Francisco, she found a good cheese source at Rainbow Grocers Co-op and Cheeseworks, in Oakland, but the truck driver from that store now comes to Santa Barbara where Olivia meets him once a month to pick up her order of parmesan reggiano. Cheese is a love of hers; she uses a great deal of it in cooking and sells it in the market. In addition, Olivia buys "back yard produce" from her neighbors if she is assured that the products have not been fertilized or sprayed with chemicals.

At the opposite end of the buying program is the composting of food scraps. She estimates the total at about 20 gallons, or 160 pounds, per day.

⌒∽

In order to keep up with current market trends and product offerings, Olivia and Steve attend trade shows. They believe that the three best trade shows are:

- The Natural Products Expo in Anaheim, California, geared toward natural food stores and organic co-ops

- The Eco-Farm Conference, sponsored by the Ecological Farm Association; a place for farmers to meet and talk farming

- The Fancy Food Show in San Francisco, good for learning about new organic products.

They advertised in the local newspaper for the first seven years until they decided that most of the locals already knew they existed. They continue an ad in the phone book but Olivia found that more and more people are relying on the internet. Therefore it is essential for them to have a website and know how to add content to it. This is particularly important because of Olivia's changing menus.

Their marketing program demanded that they become web savvy and register with such sites as The Happy Cow—a vegetarian restaurant review website—and with general (not only vegetarian) business review sites such as YELP, Trip Advisor, BooRah and Local Harvest, a CSA and farms networking site.

Because The Farmer and The Cook is a niche operation, Steve and Olivia received media attention from Huffington Post, Sunset Magazine, Automobile Club of America and other publications. As a result, Olivia comments, "the advantage to being a niche is that locals and tourists alike seek us out. We attract customers who are very particular about what they eat or who have specific needs due to health problems."

The marketing direction that did not work was in 2006, when gas prices rose and forced up the price of food. Their food costs rose 20 percent but Olivia did not feel she could raise the price of a meal from $10 to $12.

There is a saying in the restaurant business that 'food brings people in but wine and beer allow one to stay in business.' They acquired a license to sell both and also hired a musician to play on weekends.

But the bad news: they had "inadvertently attracted drunken crowds of party animals," Olivia explained, "and the customers walked out on their bills." From grossing $300 a night they jumped to $1,800. Their small kitchen could not handle that volume of business: the café was too small, the service too slow, and the wait staff did not know to which tables the orders were to be delivered (after that, Olivia assigned table numbers).

They had serious problems. Initially they invested about $20,000 plus credit cards, which they maxed out, explains Olivia, "and I would say we have just now turned the corner of barely getting by." But they are confident they have moved in the right direction.

Torn between their ability to now pay their bills, but knowing they had made mistakes serving wine and beer and not limit the clientele to what their kitchen could handle, they knew a return to their health-conscious philosophy and business was mandatory.

The café has since evolved into a community hangout where locals gather regularly to eat their daily farm-to-table fare including her baked goodies. Doubling as a market, but with take-out items added, the café features home grown produce and specialty dishes prepared with ingredients such as preserved Meyer lemons and chipotle-lime salt, among others.

In the end, on the road to becoming debt free they were able to expand the café by building a large outdoor dining area and, most important to them, they clarified their own intent and moved on.

Olivia relates the following story:

"For the first five years of the business, I was the primary cook, which was fine when we were small. But when we grew, it was very stressful. I would be stirring a pot of soup, talking to someone in accounts payable and training a new employee all at the same time. I didn't have the satisfaction of a job well done and I would go home every night with throbbing feet.

"During this last year some amazing employees—we seem to attract lovely people—have come into our lives and taken on major organizational tasks. We went on vacation last summer and when we came back our offices had been completely redone, with new desks, new hanging folder file cabinets, and bulletin boards. It is very easy to assume that no one else can do the scheduling, but in fact there is probably someone out there who can do a better job than you can.

"Because of this I have been able to return to the kitchen. For instance, this morning I made two apple pies and was only interrupted five times. Our goal is truly to be the farmer and the cook."

✑

There are not many organic bakeries in full operation around the country today. Some organic food stores carry a few packaged selections but perusing labels for ingredient contents, one notices at least one non-organic item on the list. GMO (Genetically Modified Organisms) products are no-nos for people who want only truly authentic organic food.

Olivia's small bakery, which is part of The Farmer and The Cook market, is one of the few 100 percent organic bakeries where the owner allows all ingredients to be published. "Our most popular dessert by far," proclaims Olivia, "is chocolate raspberry cake." Like the Mexican Wedding Cake (actually a cookie) the cake and its frosting are made dairy-free by using coconut oil instead of butter with the same rich result. Olivia's philosophy is, "If you want to eat a low-fat dessert have an apple, but don't take the butter [or in this case coconut oil] out of a cookie," and she adds, "everything you eat should taste delicious."

Asked if she had ever experienced one of the inevitable baker's uh-oh moments such as accidentally using salt instead of sugar in a recipe, she admitted it has happened, and further revealed that once they accidentally put garlic-infused oil into the sourdough pancakes—but that doesn't sound too bad, does it?

The Farmer and The Cook bakery makes two breads every day for use in the café and for sale in the market. The ingredients of grain and seed spelt bread are whole spelt flour, white spelt flour, sunflower seeds, golden flax seeds, rolled oats, starter, yeast, and sea salt. Sourdough rye bread contains rye flour, rye berries, rolled oats, sunflower seeds, sesame seeds, starter, and sea salt.

Muffins and other baked goodies are pleasingly displayed in antique wooden bakery cases.

The following represent both the new (since The Farmer and The Cook opened) and 'old' recipes, from Olivia's Ventura bakery, several of which are presented each day and at least one from each group.

Organic ingredient foods are just that. Anyone with health problems like dairy allergies, for example, may not be able to eat any of the goodies in this group despite their healthful, organic ingredients; nor are they recommended for people who may be trying to lose weight.

Lemon Bars contain white spelt flour, powdered sugar, butter, lemon extract, sugar, eggs, lemon zest, lemon juice and baking power.

Choco Nut Cookies contain butter, brown sugar, white sugar, eggs, white spelt flour, baking soda, salt, vanilla and chocolate chips.

Cream Cheese Swirl Brownies contain whole spelt flour, white spelt flour, sugar, almonds, anise seed, orange zest, eggs, vanilla extract, baking sold, and salt.

∽

Gluten-free foods are fine for one who cannot, or choose not, to ingest gluten or wheat.

Little Coconut Macaroons contain coconut flakes, sweetened condensed milk, chocolate chips and vanilla.

Peanut Butter Cookies contain peanut butter, sugar, eggs, sea salt, and chocolate chips.

∽

Vegan foods contain no animal products making them ideal not only for vegetarians, but also for non-vegetarians with dairy allergies or lactose intolerance. Olivia prepares delicious—and hard-to-find—vegan bakery treats such as these:

Molasses Chews are made from whole spelt flour, baking soda, salt, cinnamon, cloves, ginger, sugar, oil and molasses.

Mexican Wedding Cakes contain white spelt flour, powdered sugar, brazil nuts, vanilla extract and coconut oil.

Coconut Domes contain coconut, coconut milk, sugar, flour, flax seed, vanilla extract, salt, chocolate chips and coconut oil.

Oatmeal Raisin Cookies contain oats, white spelt flour, whole spelt flour, baking soda, date sugar, earth balance (a vegan version of 'margarine') and raisins.

Oatmeal Chocolate Chip Cookies contain oats, white spelt flour, whole spelt flour, baking soda, date sugar, earth balance and chocolate chips

Raspberry Oat Bars contain raspberries, sugar, cornstarch, oats, whole spelt flour, brown sugar, baking soda, salt and oil.

Peach Oat Bars contain peaches, sugar, cornstarch, oats, whole spelt flour, brown sugar, baking soda, salt and oil.

Strawberry Oat Bars contain strawberries, sugar, cornstarch, oats, whole spelt flour, brown sugar, baking soda, salt, and oil.

❧

Bakery treats that are both vegan and gluten-free are a good choice not only for vegetarians but also people with dairy-, wheat- and gluten-restricted diets. They offer a maximum of exotic flavors and textures from spices, seeds and fruits, with a minimum of calories; and are high in natural fiber.

Raw Coconut Caramel Wafers contain coconut, dates, almond butter, agave syrup, cinnamon, nutmeg, salt and vanilla extract.

Raw Bliss Balls contain walnuts, figs, dates, prunes, coconut flakes, cacao nibs, hempseeds, gogi berries, carob powder, mesquite powder, cranberry, cinnamon, nutmeg, maca powder and coconut oil.

Raw "Caschew" Balls contain almonds, cashews, dates and raisins

Raw Brownies contain cocoa nibs, coconut oil, almond butter, dates, cinnamon, vanilla extract, agave syrup and walnuts

❧

Vegan choices, with honey (mentioned because some vegans choose not to consume honey) are astonishingly rich and flavorful while remaining dairy- gluten- and wheat-free, besides being 'sugar' free.

Raw Cocoa Balls are gluten-free and contain cocoa nibs, coconut oil, cashews, mesquite powder, honey, cinnamon and vanilla extract.

Peanut Butter Bars have a graham cracker crust (made with wheat flour; therefore not gluten-free), oil, honey, peanut butter and chocolate chips.

Bird Feeder Cookies are gluten-free and made with raspberries, honey, oats, soy oil, raisins, sesame seeds, almonds and cinnamon.

❧

The Farmer and The Cook encompasses several aspects of a food business picture: Olivia, the cook, with her country-style retail market, comfortable farmhouse-style indoor café and large outdoor café; and Steve, the farmer, as a wholesaler of his farm's prize-winning produce, as well as a distributor through his CSA program. Add to that an online shop, a cook's organic recipe blog and a farmer's organic agriculture commentary and the result is an organic food enterprise that begins at the earth and reaches out to the world.

The Farmer and The Cook
339 West El Roblar
Ojai, California 93023
Phone: (805) 646-0960
farmerandcook1@gmail.com
www.farmerandcook.com

PFUND'S MOLKEREI

Across the Elbe River from the old city of Dresden, Germany, is Neustadt, the new city. The distinction is important because only the latter was relatively spared by British and American bombs during World War II, even though the Communists had left, both the old and the new city were in tatters. Pfund's Molkerei, or Dairy, founded in 1879, remained in existence until 1978, was reborn in 1993, and today is considered so special and unique that Guinness Book of World Records has included it every year since 1998 as the world's most beautiful dairy store.

And the entire operation is green.

The founder, Paul Gustav Leander Pfund, and his wife moved to Dresden with six cows in 1879. Paul, a dairy farmer, insisted it was of utmost importance to sell clean, hygienic milk in a store—his store—instead of buying it daily from open, poorly cooled wagons in a small nearby village.

Paul's customers could watch him milk the cows and twice filter it through fine cheesecloth. Then he cooled and delivered the milk himself.

Paul was progressive; common sense drove his decision-making. Business grew, and he moved to the dairy's current location, parallel to the river at the edge of the tourist route—today in an area of upstart green businesses—close to the trolley where tourist buses park, and where parking lots dot the landscape.

He became known with the help of his brother, Frederich, a charming actor and a magnet for many important customers. But his brother died young.

Paul enlisted his sons, Max and Kurt, to "build an empire" with new technology that produced cleaner milk—and more of it. His greatest success, however, was the introduction of pasteurized milk in 1900. He then expanded into production of condensed milk and even milk soap.

The three of them cared deeply about social issues, especially those concerning their employees, and began to expand with furnished housing, a spa, a kindergarten, health insurance, and rooms for the growing workforce. They added a factory to build wagons (in the beginning, for milk delivery), a carpentry shop, a blacksmith for 100 horses, and later, after Paul died in 1923, a carton factory and a printing facility to produce advertisements in many languages, sometimes for inclusion in books and guides about Dresden, which the company also printed.

Max, who took over the business, added a bottle and can factory, a construction company, business offices, a painting department, a train, state-of-the-art sterilization equipment, tailors for the workers' uniforms, and a pig farm for sausage production.

Max and his son, Paul, fervently carried on the essentially green philosophy and traditions of the founder. All products—including cream, many kinds of cheese, yogurt, kefir, buttermilk and powdered milk—were chosen with this in mind: "We work together for quality and care" and a logo that declared, "Taking care of the big city with milk." Max died in 1950.

Great grandson Paul Frederich Pfund directed the entire operation from that time on until his death in 1978, the Communist era, when the dairy produced 63,400 quarts of milk a day. After that time, the enterprise fell into disrepair.

Dr. Frank Zabel bought the property in 1993 from the Communist government. It took five years—two just to assemble the artisans—to restore the main enterprise, Pfund's Molkerei, to its original 1906 condition (the Communist regime prohibited renovations).

Frank not only restored the colorful, intricately-designed 60 square miles of glass ceilings and tiled flooring, but also nine-and-a-half square miles of exquisite Villeroy and Boch tiles made in a Meissen Factory. The tiles cover the surrounding walls, hallways, counters, columns and window panels and line the large mirrors.

Elegant food hall of Pfund's Molkerei in Dresden, Germany.

Like a fairy tale, the vivid colors of the hand-painted tiles depict not only children, flowers, butterflies, animals and insects in bucolic settings—much like the countryside in the early 20th century—but the presentation of milk to babies, a horse-drawn milk wagon, and milk bottles and two cans of condensed milk with the phrase, "Milk for children and the sick," as a symbol of the Pfund philosophy.

In addition to replicating the dairy's elegant, renaissance-style interior, Frank adheres to the progressive Pfund philosophy and traditions, and adds to them.

Locals and visitors can pour a glass of fresh milk or buttermilk from two huge milk cans. They can also contribute to help restore the old milk well from which guests will be able to draw a glass—no plastic, Frank emphasized—as it was in 1910.

Today, the Molkerei specializes in cheese more than milk, although it does produce the latter, but mostly in cans of condensed milk. There are also milk chocolates, candies, jams, milk soap, mugs, cheese cutters and tools, and Dresden-area books and guides. A house specialty is the popular drink called Milkgrappa (a highly alcoholic brandy made from grape skins, stems and seeds—leftovers from winemaking). The store sells a great amount of Milkgrappa. Frank touts these products as top-sellers, as are Miessen (a nearby town) wines. He intends to add other local wines; meanwhile, the Miessens offer a Weiss burgundy, reisling, rosé and dornfelauer, a local specialty.

All cheeses are made with milk from cows, goats and sheep. Frank's partner, Wilfried Hensel, went to trade fairs and traveled for two years to small towns in Switzerland, Italy, France and Spain, as well as East and West Germany, to identify small cheese farmers and makers who would sign exclusive contracts with the Molkerei. The farmers could produce a variety of some of them for only 10 other shops, which must be at least 200 miles from Dresden, according to the contracts.

The selection of cheeses is fabulous: more than 115 original varieties and always looking for new sources.

The company emphasizes free-range animals and "organic" feed. It makes cheese from raw milk, which is not heated, in order to achieve the best flavor and health benefits. Frank favors only aged cheese.

He created Pfund's cheese-specialty restaurant, located atop the store with seating for up to 90 people—cozy, but with ample space for groups and seminars. One of his initiatives involves renting buses to bring tourists for cheese tastings from large cities such as Cologne. Pfund serves special cheeses from local sources with specialty cheesecake and Quark, a sour cream-like base with various fruits or nuts or other additions that is a German specialty.

Frank imparted a bit of his philosophy when, speaking of his personnel, he declares, "Good-looking people absolutely are able to sell more."

Frank Zable is a man of great enthusiasm, great charm and pragmatic ideas, like the founder, Paul Pfund. He always has an idea or two in mind for the future and a few in the works now. There is no doubt in his demeanor that every good idea will come to fruition. He is a man of great confidence, a visionary, like the founder.

He will not pay for advertisements or promotions. In the beginning, he said, he had no money. It took every penny to restore the ruins. He asked the tourism board to promote the dairy gratis in its brochures. The board said no.

Frank found other ways to promote his enterprise. One of the first was the best marketing tool of all: distinctive bags—a child in a Villeroy and Boch tile, enlarged—that people could identify from a block away. He introduced promotions of Pfund's Molkerei reproductions and wall decorations. He instituted policies for gift-wrapping (an outstanding method of advertising) and for shipping products worldwide—even before he created an online shop.

Gift items are designed and made with the tile motifs especially for the Internet shop. Catalogs are another promotional vehicle. And Frank is studying the development of milk-based food, cosmetics, and even medicinal preparations, such as milk of magnesia.

Seizing an opportunity when it presents itself or quick thinking for free publicity, Frank told the following story:

> "The circus came to Dresden when Wilfried Hensel was there with his daughter during the Christmas season some years ago. A beautiful young lady was riding a cow into a manger setting. Afterward, Wilfried approached her to ask if she would be willing to bring the cow to the Molkerei. He would ask permission of circus officials if she consented, which she and they did. He told the officials that he would inform the press of the event, generating publicity for the circus and the store.

"Every member of the Dresden press wanted to cover the story, it turned out, and they were pushing each other to be in front, inside Pfund's. Along came the beautiful young lady wearing a gorgeous dress, sitting regally on the cow, with the press yelling at her to 'ride the cow into the shop,' and they wanted her to feed cheese to the cow." Frank told them he couldn't allow that for health reasons. But they badgered him and badgered him, every reporter and every photographer. So he finally consented.

"The resulting photo appeared on the front page in every paper in Dresden and in several other newspapers—the girl on Elsa, the cow, feeding her cheese. The first sentence of one paper read, 'Elsa the cow was well educated, a lady; not a bull in a porcelain shop'."

Following the great publicity, customers came from far and wide, and most might have never known that Pfund's Molkerei had reopened for business.

The dairy store has become a destination in itself.

Pfund's Molkerei
Bautzner Strasse 79
01099 Dresden
Germany
Phone: 011-0351-8160
info@pfunds.de
www.pfunds.de

ORGANIC BABY FOOD

t is amazing to find so many certifications of organic baby food in the United States alone, but to find companies in countries like South Africa is to understand just how important organic baby food is for a multitude of reasons. From baby health problems to lifelong allergies to the beginning of adult diseases that develop very slowly, organic food is not infrequently what makes the difference.

∽

Some words and acronyms need explanation such as the USDA—United States Department of Agriculture—that oversees the National Organic Program; in turn, NOP established the criteria for the certification of organic food in the United States.

"Certified Organic" refers to products that have first met guidelines, then received certification to use the term "organic" in product labeling. In this country, certified organic foods fall into four categories, from highest to lowest: "100% Organic," "Organic," "Made with Organic Ingredients" and "Other."

No food product that carries the USDA Organic label contains chemicals such as herbicides or fungicides, used to kill pests. These substances are toxic, used in conventional farming and show up in most conventional food products.

To acquire a 100 percent organic certification, baby food will not contain:

- Additives—substances, natural or synthetic, added to preserve or enhance freshness, flavor and color (vinegar, salt, sweeteners, dyes, sulphur dioxide, thickeners are common additives)

- Fillers—excessive use of sugars, flours, rice and other modified starches

- Preservatives in the form of nitrates, which are synthetic

- Freezing is a natural preservative and salt, sugar and vinegar, while preservatives, might be acceptable in a children's food labeled "other."

✑

HAPPYBABY is USDA 100 percent organic certified. Shazi Visram, the founder and CEO, and Jessica Rolph, founding partner and COO —two mothers who shunned the limited choices of fresh baby food—started the company in New York City in 2006. They have the first premium baby brand in the city. Their products are sold in 5,000 stores in the United States. They offer five different lines to major retailers around the country with their frozen varieties offered to grocery chains such as Whole Foods, for example, and the cereals to Amazon.

HAPPYBABY frozen foods consist of Simple Purees, Smooth Combos and Sorta Chunky for babies younger than 1 year; HAPPYBELLIES consist of organic brown rice, oatmeal and multigrain cereals, and HAPPYBITES are frozen toddler meals, fruits and vegetables.

There are 43 varieties of HAPPYBABY products in all with gluten-free puffs the latest variety. (www.happybabyfood.com)

✑

Gluten is a major protein found in wheat, barley, and rye. It is difficult for some adults to digest, but for many babies it could be the start of a lifelong intestinal problem because it can damage the lining of the small intestine. Most organic baby food is gluten-free.

DHA—docosahexaenoic acid—is a fatty acid sometimes added to cereals and later stage meals (as HAPPYBABY does). The role of DHA is to support brain and eye development in babies.

Yummy Spoonfuls and its founder and CEO Agatha Achindu is an impressive story. One might even think it is the perfect organic baby food company. Located in Atlanta, Georgia, it has already produced 25 foods—with another two currently in the works—since 2006. In fact, Agatha adds several new products per year.

The business started in the kitchen of her house some years before she and her husband had their first child. Friends, coworkers and family members asked her to convert favorite recipes into organic, nutritious meals. Soon she became an organic star chef for dinner parties, which became the hottest events in her community.

In fact, the words "nutritious organic junkie" come to mind, as Agatha—who started cooking at age 9 on the farm where she grew up in Cameroon, Africa—knew only organic fruits and vegetables that her family grew. As she grew older, and with an open mind, she experimented with different tastes, foods, and consistencies to expand the palate of those for whom she cooked.

She became so passionate about nutrition, even before her business and baby were born, that she developed workshops and traveled around the country conducting nutrition seminars to parents groups and organizations, which she continues today.

Yummy Spoonfuls is divided into three stages. Creamy Yummy (4 to 9 months), which includes seven single ingredient pureed foods, three fruits and four vegetables. Mushy Yummy (9 to 12 months) consists of 11 mostly mashed combinations such as carrot, potato and parsnip; dried apricot and rice cereal, blueberry and millet cereal; blueberry and banana cereal; papaya, quinoa and banana; garden fresh medley and the single-ingredient mashed mango. Chunky Yummy (12 months and up) consists of four combinations with more additions in the works: adzuki beans and sweet potato porridge, potato porridge, lentil and carrot porridges and rice medley.

Yummy Spoonfuls is 100 percent USDA certified through the certifying agency Organic—part of the Georgia Crop Improvement Association Organic Certification Program (GCIAOCP). Agatha will use only suppliers that comply with Fair Trade laws, and then accepts only certified-organic items. Every meal is prepared and made according to the Hazard Analysis and Critical Control Program (HACCP), the strictest safety system that exists, implemented by the FDA.

Containers are BPA-free.

Yummy Spoonfuls can be found in select Atlanta grocers, can be shipped from Amazon to anywhere in the continental United States and is also sold through its website.

Agatha Achindu, Chief Yummy Officer, summarizes this way: "Feeding our children is the first, most basic thing we do as parents. Organic foods are a step on the path to lasting health both for children and adults and for the planet." (www.YummySpoonfuls.com)

⁌

The most unique part of Jack's Harvest in Roswell, Georgia, is founder Heather Schoenrock's signature heart-shaped "cubes" of frozen organic baby food. Heather is in partnership with her brother, Joseph House. She has been cooking since she was a teenager so it was natural for her to create and perfect new recipes when cooking for her three young children.

Not only are Jack's Harvest products USDA-certified organic, but also every food item is certified 100 percent organic by the GCIAOCP.

Heather is a firm believer in introducing herbs and spices early. Flavors, she believes, are enhanced with spices such as cinnamon, citrus, mint, ginger and, further, have natural medicinal benefits along with their extra nutrients. So smooth, single-ingredient foods have a dash of cinnamon, for instance, added to broccoli; a bit of mint to peas; a pinch of ginger to carrots. This category consists of four fruits and three vegetables shipped in one-ounce cubes.

A Little Lumpy foods are flavorful combinations of two or more fruits and/or vegetables such as butternut squash with apples and a touch of sage. The group consists of three varieties and is shipped in three-ounce cubes.

Started in 2008, Jack's Harvest is another company that can be shipped via Amazon, in 12-ounce resealable bags and also can be found in certain grocers throughout Georgia. (www.JacksHarvest.com)

෴

Gerber, the highest profile brand name in baby foods, was never known as organic, but in 2006, it introduced its first item in its organic line that totals 33 varieties and continues to increase. Gerber First Foods consist of seven fruits—one of which is prunes—and 13 vegetables; Gerber Second Foods consist of 17 purees of fruits and vegetables and three cereals with fruit. Twelve combination foods are for babies from 3 months to a year old. Gerber Third Foods, that consist of two different dinners, one of which is chicken and vegetable ravioli, are their latest additions along with two different types of cereal. Gerber's newest category, juice, offers two different kinds. The company expects to develop more varieties in these three categories. Some varieties are fortified with DHA.

Gerber's operations are located in Arkansas and Michigan, but certification is under one umbrella, USDA Certified Organic.

Gerber can be purchased on Amazon as well as in most grocery store chains. Its packaging consists of glass jars, boxes, and plastic containers of which the inner layer is BPA-free; the middle layer is pure oxygen and the outermost layer is also BPA-free plastic. (www.gerber.com)

෴

BPA is Bisphenol-A, an organic compound found in many plastic food containers. Excessive use of it can cause health problems, some experts say. As a result, in 2008, many baby product manufacturers began making food containers and bottles with BPA-free plastics.

∽

Earth's Best, another very large organic baby food company was started in 1985 by two brothers from Vermont. The company (which also carries pet food products) is now located in Boulder, Colorado. In 1987, the organic food processing facility opened with only seven fruit and two vegetable purees. In 2000, The Hain Celestial Group purchased Earth's Best. There are approximately 74 foods, including formulas, in production.

Earth's Best is certified organic by Oregon Tilth, an exacting agency accredited by the USDA, meaning that the company can display the USDA Organic logo on its packaging. In addition, all food products, except those containing meat, comply with Kosher regulations.

For infants, there are three types of cereals in boxes, two of which have fruits added, in addition to jars of single fruits. Second Foods, for babies 6 months and older, include fruit and grain combinations and antioxidant blends consisting of special combinations, such as apple, turkey and cranberry, and juices. Third Foods for babies 9 months and older include chunkier fruits and soups in combinations such as carrot and tomato, banana and mango, and sweet potato and apricot.

A number of Sesame Street-brand goods were developed for toddlers and kids in addition to individual juice boxes and whole grain crackers and bars. Earth's Best and Sesame Street became partners in 2004 and the result is approximately 24 products including Sesame Street Breakfasts, Sesame Street Meals—soups, pizza and frozen entrees, for example—and Sesame Street Snacks.

Earth's Best is so complete a company of organic baby food that it offers an infant formula and two types of 2 percent reduced fat milk: original and chocolate milk. And in its latest major move, in 2008, Earth's Best introduced a line of baby care products, which completes its babies-to-kids picture. (www.earthsbest.com)

∽

World Baby Foods, or Dr. Susanna's World Baby Foods, is interesting for two reasons. One is that the six organic products were devised by two physicians, Dr. Susanna Block and Dr. Jonathan Scheffer, a husband-and-wife team; the other is their motive in creating the company which is based in Seattle, Washington, where they live and practice.

That motive started when as doctors they worked with the International Medical Corps, Doctors Without Borders and the Navajo people in Asia, Africa, Latin America as well as in parts of the United States. Health and their deep interest in world cultures and their foods led Susanna, a pediatrician, and Jonathan, a family medicine practitioner, to create a way for children to experience the broadening effects of culture—through foods.

These six varieties are certified organic by the Washington State Department of Agriculture:

Baby Dal offers a taste of India, blending lentils, rice, carrots and apples with cumin.

Baby Borscht introduces the flavors of Eastern Europe by combining beets, carrots, potatoes, spinach and dill.

Tokyo Tum Tum combines the oriental flavors of ginger, soy, brown basmati rice and apple.

Lullaby Thai made with the flavors of Thailand, are a combination of jasmine rice, and bananas with a dash of turmeric.

Que Pasa Calabasa, with its Spanish flavor combinations, blends squash, potatoes and garbanzo beans lightly seasoned with sweet mild chili.

The two physicians' desire to promote cultural understanding and health through organic nutritionally balanced meals, richly varied in ingredients and flavors, is their number one goal. (www.worldbabyfoods.com)

≈

Quality Assurance International (QAI) is a global organization that provides organic certification services and the

National Organic Program. Many baby food companies attain certification for their products through this organization.

❧

In New South Wales, Australia, a group of parents with 11 'bubs' (children) between them, joined forces to start an organic baby food concern, Organic Bubs. With three directors—one is an organization/production manager, another a marketing director, and the third a manager of everything else—plus a nutritionist and a parenting adviser, they opened for business in 2006.

Organic Bubs "tubs for bubs" come in seven varieties, including unusual flavor combinations such as corn, pumpkin and chia. Organic "pouch packs" come in apple and berry bircher muesli; vegetable rice congee; and blueberry, banana and quinoa.

All foods are certified by Australian Certified Organic (ACO).

Organic Bubs can be found in many stores throughout Australia or they can be ordered via their website for home delivery. (www.organicbubs.com)

❧

Soil Association Certification Ltd. This organization certifies up to 80 percent of the United Kingdom's organic products.

❧

What a coup! In 2006, So Baby, a frozen organic baby food company in the United Kingdom was awarded a Gold Organic Food Award from the Soil Association. Three years later, the Soil Association and the prestigious (London) Times awarded So Baby "Best Baby and Children's Meal of 2009." (This would be equivalent to the USDA and The New York Times giving such an award.)

Among the 11 varieties of main meals and two kinds of desserts are some gluten- and dairy-free vegetarian and vegan selections. All are prepared and tested by parents and babies in their organic kitchen on a small farm in Cheshire, England.

So Baby devised a child's version of the quintessential English national dish "cottage pie:" organic lean minced (ground) beef and seasonal vegetables in beef stock with "hand piped" mashed potatoes around the container's edge.

Other interesting combinations are spaghetti bolognese with small spaghetti strands and a beef, vegetable and stock sauce; salmon and vegetable pie (fresh salmon in a cheese and leak sauce); Moroccan lamb with cous cous; and fruity oat pot with apples, apricots, sultanas (raisins) and creamy organic oats—a combination for dessert, or a breakfast alternative.

So Baby products are found in the United Kingdom in organic food stores, delis and farm shops, or they will take phone or online orders.

Kudos to this small innovative company. (www.so-baby.co.uk)

∽

HiPP Organic is one of the largest organic baby food companies in the world. Founded by the Hipp family in Germany in 1899, it was situated in Berkshire, England, by 1995 and became the largest organic baby food company in the United Kingdom. Georg, son of the founder, started the baby food operation in 1932; in 1956, he converted the family farm into one of the first organic farms in Europe.

Their environmental beliefs do not extend to organic food alone; their offices, kitchens and production facilities are green as well. They are certified by European Union Standards and by Soil Association Certification Ltd.

From HiPP's fields of vegetables to the fruits in their orchards and milk from their dairy farm, through cooking and production, every product endures up to 260 quality control tests.

Categories of their 127 products are:

- Stage 1: from 3 months, more than 50 varieties of breakfasts, desserts and savouries

- Stage 2: from 7 months, more than 30 varieties of breakfasts, desserts and savoury meals

- Stage 3: from 10-12 months, more than 20 varieties of meals, finger foods and desserts

- Stage 4: from 15 months, more than 12 varieties of full meals

- Milk: three varieties to fill nutritional gaps for infants and toddlers

- Drinks: more than 12 varieties of drinks juices and smoothies

Examples of their recipes include Mediterranean potato and lamb; penne with tomato and courgette; and mango and banana with yogurt.

Besides the United Kingdom, one can buy their products online and at select retailers. HiPP Organic products are sold at select grocers in 47 countries.

What a fine green business! (www.hipp.co.uk)

∽

Genetically Modified Organisms (GMOs) are organisms whose genetic makeup has been altered using genetic engineering techniques. In the United States, corn, soy and cotton are the top three genetically engineered crops. These staples appear as corn syrup, soybean oil and cottonseed oil in many ingredient lists. Organic foods contain no GMOs.

∽

Holle, whose facilities and headquarters are located on the Swiss-German border, is a distributor and preparer of organic baby food throughout Europe, Australia and New Zealand. The company, since its 1933 inception, has always been an organic baby food manufacturer.

Infant milk formulas and grain varieties such as cereals, crackers and biscuits are produced in Germany; baby food products, in Switzerland; rice, in Italy; and millet, in Hungary.

All are soy-free and many are gluten-free. Holle has European Union certification.

The full cream milk used for the four infant formulas (one of which is goats milk) comes from dairy farms in the German Alps and Austria run by farmers who are certified organic by Demeter. Grains in cereals also originate from German farms. There are six varieties of cereal and formulas in boxed containers, and two types of tea, one a kids' tea and one for nursing mothers, a spelt rusk (a teething biscuit), a cookie and two flavors of fruit bars also with ingredients colorfully pictured on the label.

The jars of 11 different fruits and vegetables are labeled with large pictures of all the fruits and vegetables contained within. It is very effective.

With the exception of one kind of tea (for nursing mothers), all of the above products are for babies. There are also five toddler products.

Altogether, Holle is an impressive operation; baby food is only one division of the company—there are others, all devoted to organic food and other products.

In 2001, two fathers, passionate about health and organic food, discussed how they could implement their idea of creating an organic baby food company—and incorporate their many beliefs into the project. One father, Leonard, with his wife, Melissa, insisted that their baby be brought up with foods they prepared themselves. The other father, Thys, founded his own health clinic and was involved with sustainable living projects. (www.holle.com.au)

In 2006, their company, Olli, opened for business. Leonard had been an organic food products buyer—a job he loved—and continued to do for Olli. He had traveled the world visiting organic farms; now he stays close to home, in South Africa, buying from local farmers. Thys, with his engineering background, is head of production in their new Olli factory, where about 15 people work per shift.

Jarred products are divided into three stages, the first consisting of six varieties of single fruits and vegetables; the second, seven varieties of combinations; and the third, six varieties of meals including brown rice, lentils and combinations with millet, fruits and vegetables. A few examples of their unordinary combinations include butternut squash and marrow, and tropical fruit including mango and guava.

All foods are certified by Ecocert SA, as well as Kosher and Halaal authorities. Olli products are sold in grocery stores, baby stores and pharmacies.

Olli is involved in helping many small, disadvantaged organic farmers by guaranteeing them payment to grow more vegetables by enlarging their farms. The company is also assisting with their organic certification costs. (As Olli grows, so too will more farmers/farms.)

At the same time, Leonard and Thys have been working with the South African Council for Organic Development and Sustainability (SOCODAS) to manage the National Organic Product Initiative (NOPI) to develop organic agricultural villages, providing sustainable income—a Fair Trade operation, South African style. Olli will buy as many of their products as possible.

In these few ways, Thys and Leonard incorporate some of their beliefs into their personal view of organic living. (www.olli.co.za)

∽

A few conclusions seem obvious. One is that almost all owners of organic food companies are parents, and most, not all, are mothers who have always enjoyed cooking for themselves, their friends and family, or, who have an unusual interest in ethnic foods, and appreciation for the organic food lifestyle. And when they make the decision to go into business they combine their interests and talent—and choose the retail food business.

Almost all of the owners or CEOs advertise and market their goods exclusively on the Internet.

Finally, almost all of the companies were founded in 2006. Why? No one was able to explain.

ORGANIC PET FOOD

When considering 100 percent organic foods in general, the picture would be incomplete without looking at pet food. The proliferation of 'organic' brands, products and types of food seems endless.

Paw Naturaw, a brand of Blue Seal Feeds, offers several organic meals and treats for dogs and cats. Like all of its pet foods, Paw Naturaw tests with dogs and cats in shelters and homes—as well as with the companion animals of Paw Naturaw executives and employees. The raw-food meals must be frozen until needed. Varieties include chicken, carrots and peas; turkey, sweet potato and peas; or 100 percent chicken and 100 percent turkey offered in 2-ounce medallions, 8-ounce patties, and 12-ounce and 3-pound rolls. They are also available in a 1-pound bag of dehydrated beef, equivalent to 2 1/2 pounds of raw diet.

Cat meals consist of turkey and turkey liver, chicken and chicken liver, turkey and chicken, and chicken and mackerel. All are rich in vitamins and minerals and gluten free. Both the cat and dog meals are USDA certified.

Paw Naturaw raw-diet food, offered in half-ounce nuggets for dogs and cats, includes organic chicken formula and turkey formula. The company's organic treats for dog and cats include Bison Jerky Treats, Beef Jerky Treats, Sweet Potato Treats, Apple Treats, and a few unusual offerings: CocoTherapy Coconut Chips—dehydrated 100 percent organic coconut meat slowly baked and dried as flakes with no added sugar, salt, preservatives or chemicals.

Other companies produce organic dry dog food. Among them are Castor and Pollux, whose brand, Organix, produces Puppy Formula Dry Dog Food made with its No. 1 certified ingredient: chicken. Organix Adult Dry Dog Food includes the chicken plus brown rice, peas, carrots and flaxseed (all organic) and Adult Less Active Dry Dog Food consists of organic fruit and vegetable purees, as well as chicken.

∽

Monzie's Organic Muesli includes all organic ingredients: oats, barley, rye, quinoa, flax and sunflower seeds, kelp and carob powder, vegetable broth powder, garlic, parsley, alfalfa, and dandelions. To prepare, consumers add meat and water.

Karma Organic dry dog food offers 95 percent organic ingredients—18 of which are certified organic—and is made with whole (not dried) organic fruit and vegetables. Even the packaging is recyclable.

∽

The category of treats includes: Newman's Own Organics Dog Training Treats, which contain, in addition to chicken, oat flour and barley flour. Another company, Monzies, also makes organic dog snacks. And Grandma Lucy's prepares its organic dog treats in a bakery, not a factory. Organix Dog Cookies are made from 95 percent organic ingredients.

Another company, Planet Dog Treats, produces two kinds of treats different from any other company: Salmon Seafood Chowder and Pumpkin Pear Ginger. Neither contains soy, corn, wheat or gluten—and both aid in tartar control.

Flying Bassett Organic Super Hero Treats—sprouts of vitamins, minerals, enzymes, plant-cell calcium and vitamins, fresh liver powder, oils, lecithin and fish protein for flavor— are encased in tablets.

∽

Organix Adult and Kitten Formula Dry Cat Foods are a meat-based protein food with chicken as the primary ingredient, plus brown rice, flaxseed, barley and peas. The company's Organic Cat Treat cookie is shaped like a tiny drumstick; they have only two calories per cookie.

Another product, for cats, is CocoTherapy Virgin Coconut Oil made from organic grown coconuts in USDA-certified coconut farms.

Organic catnip, is carried by two companies: Castor and Pollux, which encases its Curious Cat catnip in vegetables, and Sojos Premium Organic catnip, which requires only a pinch of the hand-harvested chopped greens once or twice a week to induce 'a harmless euphoric state' in cats that lasts five to 15 minutes.

∽

Only one product, good for pets of all kinds, from ponies to rabbits, can be grown at home: Pet Greens Organic Wheat Grass Garden—organic greens that grow out of the bag they come in.

∽

For the potential pet food business owner, the products above represent a sampling of the available product variety and demonstrate the dramatic expansion of the organic pet food industry.

CHAPTER 9

BIOPLASTICS

For decades scientists have been competing to find a solution to the problem of plastic waste. Petroleum- and chemical-based plastics add to a dependence on oil, cause damage to animals and the environment, and take hundreds of years to degrade, creating overflow in U.S. landfills faster than new landfills can be found.

The solution—fortuitously for the planet—is bioplastics, derived from plants such as hemp, jute, corn, soy, starch, yams, peas, wheat, sugarcane, and even oranges.

Research shows the long-term benefits of 100 percent bioplastics are:

- 100 percent natural with no chemical elements added
- 100 percent biodegradable and compostable
- carbon-neutral

The list of products that can be produced by bioplastics is extremely promising, and an impressive list of major corporations and industries are using bioplastic materials in scores of products: auto parts; packaging for everything from cosmetics to fresh produce; construction; gift cards; containers; and what used to be called plastic ware (plates, cups, bowls, etc.) The main drawback, however, is that 100 percent bioplastic products tend to be costly and unable to maintain their integrity over many years. But, as with most new technology, costs will drop as bioplastic products become popular with consumers.

In addition to plants, industrialized countries around the world, including the United States, China, Sweden, the United Kingdom, and Europe, are pursuing research that can turn shrimp shells, lactic acid, algae and a variety of what used to be considered garbage into fuel additives, industrial lubricants, insecticides, and more. The technology is creating products so quickly that today's technical information will be outdated tomorrow.

It's safe to say that bioplastics will be one of the most important green developments of this century, one that entrepreneurs considering a retail, wholesale, or Internet business should consider.

If bioplastics intrigues you, begin your research on the Internet, where you can find, books, magazines, technical information, awards, conferences, and trade shows devoted to bioplastic technology.

OLIVE GREEN MARKETING

Aloysius Cheong, owner of Olive Green Marketing (OGM) in Singapore, is the distributor of CornWare that is manufactured in China, and will soon become a manufacturer of CornWare.

The term "distributor" can entail different responsibilities in different countries, but Aloysius' definition is: "A legal entity that does the marketing and distribution of the products within a given geographical area." He defines a wholesaler as "a distributor and a manufacturer as well." Once he becomes a manufacturer, he can achieve one of his goals: wholesaling his products anywhere—"and that includes China, the United States and Europe," he says.

Aloysius graduated college with a bachelor of science degree with two majors: economics and political science. He married in 2009, and his wife—who graduated with a business administration degree—handles the day-to-day operations of the CornWare business. Aloysius has two other ongoing business ventures: one is a Center for Tuition Services, providing teachers for mentoring school-age children; the other is a private organization involved in an eco-friendly business.

In 2005, Aloysius chanced upon the emerging industry of bioplastics. He was "captivated" by the fact that there could be a material, made from plants, which could replace petroleum-based plastics. After two years of intensive research, he realized there would be a huge international bioplastics market in future.

In 2007, he met with the relevant scientists in China who conceptualized the CornWare family of bioplastics. At that point, Aloysius needed to fund OGM's operation to set up the distributorship. The bulk of the capital came from the reserves of his two businesses and some venture capitalists who, he said, joined him to provide the "firepower" to market not only the largest group of products, CornWare, but also CornBags and CornPack, two smaller product groups. OGM is wholly owned by Aloysius and it was he who gave the name to the primary material, which became CornWare.

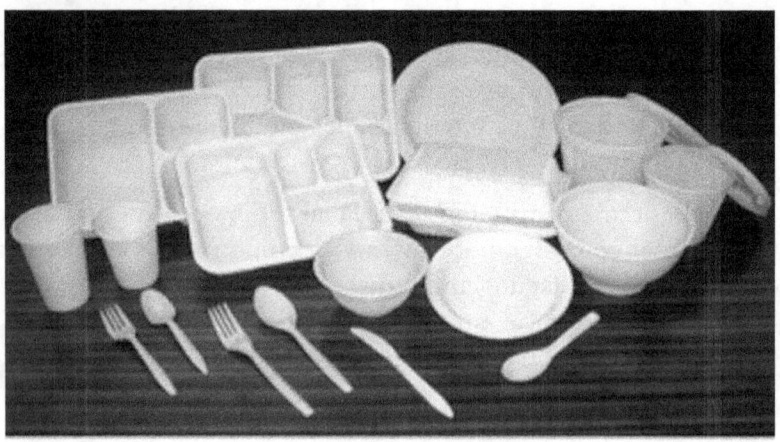

CornWare is a green alternative to polystyrene.

CornWare is made from Origo—a starch-based bioplastic made from corn and yam with polypropylene (PP) added. Aloysius concedes, "We have to include PP in order to make CornWare commercially functional and to ensure waterproofing." CornWare decomposes within 120 days.

CornWare is the green answer to polystyrene foam products, though far superior as far as green benefits—like comparing diamonds to rhinestones. Aloysius warns that certain types of polystyrene, when heated above a certain temperature, leech into food. In his opinion, drinking hot coffee for a year from polystyrene products is equivalent to consuming a cup of toxins. Edward Machuga, Ph.D., a consumer safety officer in the FDA's Center for Food Safety and Applied Nutrition, has written: "It's true that substances used to make plastics can leech into food. But as part of the approval process, the FDA considers the amount of a substance expected to migrate into food and the toxicological concerns about the particular chemical."

Additional research on this topic has found no conclusive studies as to which plastics leech into food, at what rate, and under what conditions, but it's significant that many U.S. fast food chains have stopped using polystyrene packaging.

CornWare products include three sizes of plates measuring six, seven and nine inches; five- and seven-inch spoons; six- and seven-inch forks; six- and eight-inch knives; stirrers; six- and nine-ounce cups; three sizes of bowls, five point five-, ten-, and 22-ounce soup bowls with lids; flip-cover lunch boxes and lunch boxes with lids; and lidded dinner boxes with three and four compartments. They are microwavable up to certain temperatures. Maximum microwave time is 15 minutes.

CornBags, OGM's answer to supermarket brown bags, are corn-based and eco-friendly but devised from a different formula. The same is true of CornPack, used for non-food disposable packaging (i.e. internal plastic wrapping of electronic goods).

It sells all the products in Singapore to all relevant markets, such as business corporations, food and beverage outlets, and caterers; wherever food and beverage disposable packaging is needed. OGM's in-house sales team takes the orders.

"The Internet is a good place to market all products, but that is just one part of marketing," Aloysius explains. "Most companies should be wise enough to know the benefits that the Internet can bring [but] for my industry another important aspect is the physical contact part. Customers still need that 'feel of the product' before any commitments can be made."

To that end, Aloysius will participate in a few trade shows to be organized in 2010 or 2011 (details of the shows are to be firmed up). For now, the marketing team is "available to create the needed buzz in Singapore" through all relevant media, including TV ads, editorials, articles in many Singapore newspapers and magazines, business collaborations, and events.

OGM was awarded the Green Label by the Singapore Environment Council, and received ISO accreditation for Quality Management System, Environmental Management System, and Determination of Aerobic Biodegradability. Additionally, Olive Green states that it is accredited by the British Retail Consortium Global Standard and passed stringent FDA testing of its food packaging in December 2008.

OGM is planning international distribution—another goal in the next year—as well as an online wholesale store.

Aloysius is brimming over with ideas to help decrease global warming. He feels passionate about the issue and the part he will continue to play in the future. "It would," he adds, "be my small contribution to halting global warming."

Olive Green Marketing
63 Hillview Ave., #03-08
Lam Soon Industrial Building
Singapore 669569
Phone: 6767 1301
www.olivegreen.com.sg

CHAPTER 10

IDEAS FOR ONLINE AND ON-SITE BUSINESSES

N ew businesses and old with a progressive bent continually launch distinctive niche retail shops that emphasize eco-friendly, recycled, renewed and/or repurposed products. In this section, the best practices from a variety of businesses generously share their know-how and experience to help fledgling green businesses flourish from coast to coast.

Going green requires progressive thinking in procuring merchandise and how to sell it. For example, it's easy to see why opening a traditional bookstore, stocked with only new books, would be business suicide. National-chain booksellers rule the brick-and-mortar market and websites such as Amazon.com dominate the Internet, offering instant downloads of a growing number of titles. These mega-retailers can sell at lower prices than independents.

However, a store serving a green niche—offering used and new books of current interest, like cookbooks and green subjects—can thrive as niche businesses. Tout the many newly published books on various subjects made from hemp, rice or bamboo paper. Add an online store that specializes in the categories you carry, and you have the foundation to grow the business beyond local borders.

For the retail shop, add a few interesting, comfortable used chairs and tables for reading, and displays that could also be for sale. If you have the space, consider adding a computer in a cozy corner for customers to research books.

Further, expand with a café by renting adjacent space and taking down the common wall. Keep it simple; serve only cold items prepared on premises or at your home—sandwiches, salads, and desserts along with a variety of teas and coffees. The benefits of cold items: they are ready-to-serve and generally inexpensive. And it's relatively easy to obtain a license. Use Cornware plates, glasses, cups and utensils for the all organic food and drinks. Soups prepared in a slow cooker could be added to the menu—no need for an expensive stove or a full restaurant license.

Ambience and displays are important for a bookstore café or any kind of green shop/store, yet business owners around the world believe that these scene-setting elements are superfluous. The ambience of a green business should be warm and cozy, if appropriate, achieved by outstanding displays: books on a table, desserts on interesting cake stands, for example. Props help sell the products.

⁂

Hardware stores represent another type of business that can go green. Stock such a store with used tools of every kind acquired through thrift shops, eBay, newspaper ads, inquiries in existing hardware stores and other methods. The store could tout its no-VOC paints and finishes, recycled paints, no-VOC glue, tape variety, LED light bulbs, and all kinds of gardening tools. In fact, it could be a store with a hardware side and a garden side with an attached greenhouse.

⁂

A clothing store can also be green. An entrepreneur could acquire used clothing from family and friends, garage sales, Goodwill, SPCA shops, church sales and the like. Consignment shops typically require clients to remove their items at the end of a season. Clients often opt to giving away their goods, which you can then purchase for next to nothing. Next, find someone who sews (if you don't)—a professional dressmaker, tailor or designer—and restore the items to fashionable clothes for men, women and children. With a few used sewing machines set in a cozy setting, you can display the clothing in an interesting manner such as hanging them on walls with large,

216

old wooden hangers and pegs or on old wooden racks and in armoires which you could also resell.

༄

Businesses tend to sell related products in one place—items traditionally sold in separate shops. The idea is to create shops-within-a-store, similar to department stores but combining only related products. A natural add-on to your clothing store, again using an adjoining space, is a fabric shop/store with a twist: it would carry only eco-friendly fabrics, such as hemp, bamboo and organic cotton. With a few recycled sewing machine stations where customers can sew their own items for an hourly fee, this area would operate like a knitting shop where people come to learn from a salesperson. The fabric remnants from both operations could be sold for rag rugs or quilts—items gaining in popularity.

This is a surprisingly successful business.

༄

Another business concept could serve camping equipment and clothing for hikers, bikers, climbers and campers. From hemp tents to recycled, reused and new sleeping bags and backpacks, the inventory could be vast. You can procure some eco-friendly products—such as boots, shoes and apparel appropriate for outdoor sport and recreation—recycled, renewed, reused, or repurposed products, including tents, stoves, knives, computer watches, and performance gear.

A natural add-on shop might sell reused, eco-friendly sports equipment: skis, sleds, toboggans and ice skates in northern climes and surfing, scuba diving, snorkeling, water skis, racquets for tennis and other sports in southern and temperate climates.

In any locale, an add-on or separate shop could sell reused bicycles for men, women and children. It would sell tricycles, motor scooters and mountain bikes, as well as a few types of green bikes, such as one made from bamboo. The shop could include a repair operation and retail space for tools, parts, accessories and apparel for road, racing and mountain biking as well as BMX and the emerging sport of extreme cycling, popularized in ESPN's X Games.

The end result would be a green sports store—with an accompanying online store, of course.

∽

If you seek a larger, more ambitious endeavor, you might acquire an old, decrepit house with at least five bedrooms, a good-sized kitchen and dining room and a porch (which you can add later) and transform it into a bed-and-breakfast. Remodel the house using eco-friendly and sustainable materials, such as hemp; bamboo; cork; non-VOC paints, glue and finishes; the latest in green pipes and plumbing; energy-saving appliances, from water heater to radiant heating; refrigerator/freezer to washing machine and dryer; and stove, sinks and toilets. Furnish the house with recycled, repurposed and reused sofas, chairs, tables, credenzas, chests of drawers, fixtures, etc.—but only brand-new bed and bath items, such as mattresses, linens, towels (and napery for the dining area), all of which are available in hemp, bamboo, organic cotton and other eco-friendly materials.

In fact, you can convert structure other than a house; some inns used to be schools and banks. Zoning laws often allow these variances, especially when urban renewal can supplant its decay.

Ultimately, this would be an all-organic bed-and-breakfast—even in the kitchen, where, instead of traditional sugars and sweeteners, you can serve agave, stevia or honey, as well as gluten and wheat-free breads and cereals, and pastries and sweet tarts with fruits or savory vegetable tarts made with organic butter and eggs. Offer recipes made with dairy-free, salt-free, sugar-free ingredients.

Here is a recipe for a delicious breakfast drink, courtesy of Joan Smith McHenry, Carmel Valley, California:

Juice three carrots, one apple, one cucumber, two pears with seeds and stem removed. Pour ¼ cup of sparkling apple cider into a champagne flute, add fruit/vegetable juice and garnish with a slice of cucumber. Use organic ingredients if you like.

Market the business to the eco-conscious, vegans and people with specialized diets.

Your website should reflect the degree to which you can accommodate special needs while appealing to your guests who have no such demands.

An add-on, a niche in itself, would be a gift shop with the eco-friendly products used in the guest rooms; foods served in the dining room (such as your famous granola), a cookbook that includes your granola recipe, take-out snacks (including your own granola bars) and products such as soaps and lotions, soy candles, hemp sheets, bamboo towels, robes and other green goods that will remind them of your charming place each time they use them.

Patronize local sources, such as farmers markets and fairs, for handmade quilts and throws and bamboo/organic cotton knitting yarns. Buy recycled and repurposed items such as hand painted clay pots for plants and kitchen utensils, pottery breakfast-ware and etched stemmed glasses made from recycled jars.

The possibilities seem endless.

Guests want to take home memorable gifts as well as goods that may not be available where they live. The shop could also have an online retail site so guests can continue shopping from home. Depending on your locale, your green bed-and-breakfast could be a niche business with little or no competition.

∽

Another on-site and online business idea, growing in popularity, is a green gift shop incorporating one very popular item surrounded by a group of similar items. Example: At any given time, one animal motif or another is in vogue, such as cows, ducks, horses, roosters, pigs, owls and, of course, cats and dogs. Similarly, there are fruit motifs: apples, lemons, cherries, strawberries, watermelons, grapes/grapevines, olives/olive branches, etc. Offer the collectible motif in every green manner and material you can find—hemp, cork, wood, clay, wrought iron, bamboo and other sustainable materials for pottery, cookie jars, planters, sculptures, luncheon ware, potholders, mailboxes, aprons, sun-catchers, bathroom accessories, socks ... the list is endless. Create vignettes with a singular motif to create a unified environment. Alternatively, group all the cookie jars, of all designs, together. The aim is to catch the eye—or, in the case of online shoppers—appear in the immensely important search results.

∽

Create an art and frame shop. Visit thrift shops, arts and crafts festivals and websites for old paintings and new artwork using green paints and brushes. You can also find papier mâché items and mineral or sustainable-wood sculptures in these venues. Seek bamboo, hemp, and sustainable woods for making frames. An add-on could be costume jewelry made of shells, sustainable woods, eco-friendly metals, with or without unusual mineral stones, beads and other materials—a jewelry shop within a store.

∽

Create a catering business specializing in organic food. Offer menus that address dietary restrictions but also appeal to all other guests.

∽

Create a custom luxury eco-travel consultant business. There are a multitude of inexpensive eco-friendly trips, including cycling, walking, and cruises that appeal to younger people, but fewer catering exclusively to seasoned travelers— this is your target market. A business with low overhead, it can operate from your home, mostly via Internet and telephone, connecting with a travel agent who handles ticketing. You need not be a travel agent to conduct this business.

Car and driver services using hybrid or electric vehicles, along with eco-friendly guides and interpreters, are popular in many countries. Certain cruise lines travel to luxurious, eco-friendly destinations. At least one airline is as close to eco-friendly as exists, as are some public forms of transportation such as buses and trains. But the best green travel business includes arranging trips to exotic destinations with cars and drivers and luxurious eco-friendly hotels or inns.

Two effective ways to advertise are through your website and by advertising in theatre, classical music, dance and opera programs (oftentimes printed by one company). Designing your ad is easy if you use only print; however, many publications include graphic design and production at no additional charge.

Mention that you offer arrangements for the handicapped (a surprising number of people take this kind of trip). Emphasize the word 'custom' with a suggestion of a luxury eco-friendly trip you are planning. Include your e-mail address or website URL, and invite travelers to sign up for advance notice of upcoming trips or special offers.

༄

Hundreds of businesses exist that you could easily convert into green businesses. Because one business already exists does not preclude a new one in the same or similar niche. Indeed, a successful business in one area may signal a fertile customer base. Be creative. Use your imagination. And research, research, RESEARCH!

APPENDIX

RESOURCE GUIDE

GREEN BUSINESS SUCCESS STORIES

Autonomie Project, Inc.
Anne O'Loughlin
119 Braintree Street, Suite 510
Boston, MA 02134
Phone: (877) 218-9131
Fax: (617) 440-7630
www.autonomieproject.com
www.myspace.com/autonomieproject
www.facebook.com/autonomieproject

bambu
Jeff Delkin
Rachael Speth
rachels@bambuhome.com
bambuhome.com
Twitter: @bambuhome
284 Anfu Road, 2/f
Shanghai, China
Phone: (86-21) 5403-6814
Fax: (86-21) 5403-4714

Carini Lang
Joe Carini
335 Greenwich St.
New York, NY 10013
Phone: (646) 613-0497
info@carinilang.com
www.carinilang.com

Carmel Development Company
Michael Waxer
Post Office Box 450
Carmel, CA 93921
Phone: (831) 625-1066
Fax: (831) 625-6220
mlwaxer@carmeldevelopment.com
Hemp Gallery

Ray Rankin
Beatrice Rankin
PO Box 84
Belrose, NSW 2085
Australia
Phone: +61.2 8901 0375
Fax: +61.2 9975 6762
info@hempgallery.com.au
www.hempgallery.com.au

Eairth

Melissa Dizon
101 Bormaheco Condominiums
Metropolitan Avenue/Zapote Street
Makati City, Metro Manila, Philippines
U.S. Phone: (646) 479-4253
Melissa@Eairth.org
www.eairth.ph

Earthtribe

Manita Senn
Phone: 0 410 619 746 (within Australia)
Phone: +61 410 619 746 (from overseas)
manita@earthtribe.com.au
www.earthtribe.com.au

Enviro International

Safwat Malek
Post Office Box 1734
Pebble Beach, CA 93953
Phone: (831) 626-3490
Fax: (831) 626-5401
SafwatMalek@enviro-international.com
www.enviro-international.com

Environment Furniture
Giovanni Gallizio and Davide Berruto
8126 Beverly Blvd.
Los Angeles, CA 90048
Phone: (323) 935-1330
Phone: (866) 981-3976
www.environmentfurniture.com

The Farmer and The Cook
Olivia Chase
Steve Sprinkel
339 West El Roblar
Ojai, California 93023
Phone: (805) 646-0960
farmerandcook1@gmail.com
www.farmerandcook.com

Ferguson
(multiple retail outlets)
1144 Fremont Blvd.
Seaside, CA 93955
Phone: (831) 394-7469
www.ferguson.com

Green Depot
(multiple retail outlets & distribution centers)
Sarah Beatty
222 Bowery
New York, NY 10012
Phone: (212) 226-0444
contactus@greendepot.com
www.greendepot.com

Green Genes
Heather Muenstermann
Christina Isperdul
5111 N. Clark St.
Chicago, IL 60640
Phone: (773) 944-9250
www.green-genes.com

GreenSky
Nadeen Kieren
5357 N. Ashland Ave.
Chicago, IL 60640
Phone: (773) 275-1911
Fax: (773) 334-1911
www.greenskycompany.com

MCA Tile
Yoshihiro Suzuki
1985 Sampson Ave.
Corona, CA 92879
Phone: (800) 736-6221
Phone: (951) 736-9590
Fax: (951) 736-6052
www.mca-tile.com

Mountains Of The Moon, LLC
Melissa Baswell
Post Office Box 25192
Chicago, IL 60625-0192
Phone: (877) 875-0689
www.mountainsofthemoon.com

MudCrafters
Talmath Lakai
Post Office Box 344
Crestone, CO 81131
Phone: (719) 256-4197
www.mudcrafters.com

The Natural Bedding Company
Andrew McCaig
122 Percival Road
Stanmore, Sydney, 2048
Phone: (02) 9569-4834
Fax: (02) 9564-6242
natbed@iprimus.com.au
www.naturalbedding.com.au

Natural Living
Ho Jai Cheung
Semmania Luk
8/F, Sungib Industrial Centre
53 Wong Chuk Hang Road
Aberdeen, Hong Kong
Phone: (852) 2847-3377
Fax: (852) 2868-5233
www.naturalliving.hk

Nest
Trine Targett
Jeff Delkin
Rachael Speth
International Artist Factory
Taikang Road, Lane 210
Studio 201 (2nd floor)
Shanghai, China
Phone: (86 21) 6466 9524
info@nestshanghai.com
nestshanghai.com

Olive Green Marketing
Aloysius Cheong
63 Hillview Ave., #03-08
Lam Soon Industrial Building
Singapore 669569
Phone: +65 6767 1301
www.olivegreen.com.sg

Pfund's Molkerei
Bautzner Strasse 79
01099 Dresden
Germany
Phone: 011-0351-8160
info@pfunds.de
www.pfunds.de

BUSINESS HELP

Service Corps of Retired Executives
SCORE
www.score.org

U.S. Small Business Association
SBA
www.sba.gov

eHow
www.ehow.com

Yahoo! Small Business
smallbusiness.yahoo.com

One Choice For Your Store
www.1choice4yourstore.com

ORGANIC BABY FOOD COMPANIES

Earth's Best
The Hain Celestial Group, Inc.
4600 Sleepytime Dr
Boulder, CO 80301
www.earthsbest.com

Gerber
445 State St
Fremont, MI 49413
www.gerber.com

HAPPYBABY
Shazi Visram
Jessica Rolph
New York City, NY
www.happybabyfood.com

HiPP Organic
United Kingdom
www.hipp.co.uk

Holle
Switzerland, Germany
www.holle.com.au

Jack's Harvest
Heather Schoenrock
Roswell, Georgia
www.JacksHarvest.com

Olli
South Africa
www.olli.co.za

Organic Bubs
New South Wales, Australian
www.organicbubs.com

So Baby
United Kingdom
www.so-baby.co.uk

Dr. Susanna's World Baby Foods
Dr. Susanna Block
Dr. Jonathan Scheffer
www.worldbabyfoods.com

Yummy Spoonfuls
Agatha Achindu
Atlanta, GA
www.YummySpoonfuls.com